in real time

in
real
time

authentic
young adult
ministry
as it
happens

MIKE GLENN

B&H
PUBLISHING GROUP
Nashville, Tennessee

978-0-8054-4694-4

Published by B&H Publishing Group
Nashville, Tennessee

Dewey Decimal Classification: 248.83
Subject Heading: YOUNG ADULTS \ CHURCH WORK
WITH YOUNG ADULTS

1 2 3 4 5 6 7 8 • 12 11 10 09

Contents

Acknowledgments

No book is ever written in a vacuum, and this one certainly wasn't. I have been writing in the midst of the joyful chaos we call ministry, both at Brentwood Baptist Church and Kairos. First of all, I want to tell the trustees and members of Brentwood Baptist Church how much I love you and how much I appreciate your support of Kairos and the time to write this book. You really are the coolest church around.

I would like to thank the leadership teams of Kairos and especially Cathy Patterson, minister to Kairos, and Michael Boggs, the worship leader of Kairos. Keely Boggs makes sure every Tuesday is ready to go. Of course, thanks to the young adults who have shared their journey with me during our Tuesday nights together. I have your faces deep in my heart. You will never know what you have done for me.

Karla Worley, my research and writing assistant, has done what she could with the mess I gave her. Please do not hold her responsible for the book's limitations. Diane Mayfield, my administrative assistant, has done her best to keep me focused and organized. I thank her for her efforts.

Last, thank you to my wife, Jeannie, who has always believed in me, even when she didn't understand what I was up to. That takes a lot, and I love her for it.

Please don't squander one bit of this marvelous life God has given us.
God reminds us, "I heard your call in the nick of time;
The day you needed me, I was there to help."
Well, now is the right time to listen, the day to be helped.

—2 CORINTHIANS 6:1–2 *The Message*

Foreword

Over the past few days, I have been engaged in a protracted discussion on the health of the American church. Perhaps, to state it more clearly, I have been engaged in a discussion on the lack of health in the American church. The conversation began with the release of the latest statistics of my denomination. They weren't pretty, and there weren't many bragging rights in the numbers.

Sometimes the conversation was a debate. Almost everyone engaged in the conversation had an opinion on why the churches in our denomination were not healthy, but no consensus emerged. Still, everyone did agree on one thing: the churches in our denomination and in our nation as a whole aren't healthy. It's too bad we had little agreement on solutions.

But, in the course of my ministry and work, I am sometimes, perhaps often, surprised by God. Just when I think things really look bad, when I believe that the cause is lost, he surprises me. I may be introduced to a ministry that is making such a tremendous impact in the inner city that I wonder why I've never heard of it. Or I may discover the work of a small, rural church that is defying all the rules by reaching dozens of people each year.

In those moments I see the hand of God.

In those moments I see that God is not yet done with his church.

The story of Brentwood Baptist Church in the Nashville metro area is a story worth telling. The church has emerged from relative obscurity to megachurch status in just a few years. The ministries are many, and the impact of the church is vast.

But this book is not the story of Brentwood Baptist Church. It is rather the story of one facet of BBC: a ministry, a church within a church, a community of believers, and a place where nonbelievers can really discover the love of Christ.

This is the story of Kairos.

For some the contrast is stark, a bit unsettling. Brentwood is the most affluent suburb of Nashville, and Brentwood Baptist often mirrors its community demographically. The facilities are vast; the multiple Sunday services are large; and the preacher wears the expected suit and tie.

But the story on Tuesday night is quite different. Mike Glenn, the senior pastor of Brentwood Baptist Church, is also the teaching pastor of Kairos. He is affectionately known as Uncle Mikey to the Kairos crowd. The perfunctory Baptist suit and tie are traded for jeans and a casual shirt. The teaching is deeply biblical, but it most often is done from a whiteboard projected onto screens around Wilson Hall, the church's large fellowship area.

The crowd at Kairos is young, urban, and postmodern. They sit at tables instead of pews. They ask questions and interject freely.

And week by week, day by day, they learn more about the love of God.

There is no pretense at Kairos. Mike and the young adults get real, many of them single and questioning the norms of life, church, and society. They quickly drop the masks of typical churchgoers and deal with tough and personal issues.

As you enter this world of Kairos, prepare to enter a world unlike most Sunday church crowds. Prepare to hear stories that will move you, maybe even change you. One of my favorites took place when Mike was teaching from the Bible about loving and honoring parents. Many in the gathering obviously tuned Mike out. So he stopped his message and asked them why they were not listening. Soon the metaphorical can of worms was opened.

One young adult speaks of hate toward his father who abandoned him and his siblings and his mother when he was young. Another young adult told of abuse by her father. And, so they asked, you want us to honor these jerks?

So many stories. So many lives changed. So real.

Kairos, a unique moment in time. Kairos, a new kind of church that may be closer to the church of two thousand years ago than most today.

Read this book. But, even more important, open your eyes and minds to how Christians are supposed to act, to care, and to love.

Yes, the American church is not healthy. But stories like Kairos give me hope because these stories remind me of the one who is the source of all hope.

You will find such hope here. And you will be surprised by God.

Prepare now to discover Kairos.

—Thom S. Rainer
President of LifeWay Christian Resources and
Brentwood Baptist Church member

Remember:
A Kairos Guided Prayer

Just Get Here

Just find a comfortable place, get both feet on the floor, take a deep breath, and say, "Hey, it's Tuesday night. It must be Kairos!"

You swore this was the week that you were going to do better with your time. This was the week you weren't going to get behind. This was the week that you would be disciplined. And it's already Tuesday. The only way you'll make it will be to add four or five days to the week. So you left the office, but you didn't leave work. You thought about it all the way over here. You sat down, got out your Blackberry, and typed a few notes, or grabbed a piece of paper to write down some things you don't want to forget, stuffed it in your pocket, and have already forgotten which pocket it's in. Oh well, the cleaners will save it for you when you take it to them.

You've got things on your mind from yesterday, things on your mind for tomorrow; but you're *here*. You can't undo anything that happened yesterday, and you can't do yet what is waiting for you tomorrow.

Jesus said, "Don't waste your time in worry." In fact, he turned to his disciples and asked, "Which one of you can grow an hour older by worry? If you can't do such a little thing like that, then don't worry about anything else" (Matt. 6:27, author paraphrase). Do you get what he said? If you could grow and

1

shrink at will, the incredible growing/shrinking man, you'd be on Letterman. But you can't do that.

So take a deep breath; close your eyes. I just want you to think about your own life, and we are going to practice *not* worrying. For some of you this will be entirely new territory. Where does it start? It starts in your memory, and I want you to spend just a few minutes remembering who God is.

Who Is God?

He's the God who created the universe. He placed Pluto so far out that the sun never warms it up. It would take you a lifetime to get out there, and that's just *our* little bitty universe, *our* little bitty galaxy, not the whole universe. Other galaxies are bigger. They are so big from end to end that you would literally have to die and be born again, then die again, and do that several hundred times for you to get across the universe from one end to the other.

He designed DNA, little bits of chemicals, atoms that communicate with one another, that figure out how tall you will be, what color hair you will have, how your voice will sound.

Did you know that Mount Everest is not the highest mountain in the world? The highest mountain in the world is at the bottom of the Pacific Ocean. It's much higher than Everest. It's just covered by a lot more water. We celebrate when someone climbs to the top of Everest. God says, "That's just a mole hill. You should see what I did in the Pacific."

Did you know that a bumblebee is not supposed to be able to fly? The size of its wings and the mass of its body don't fulfill the aerodynamics principles we understand. But God tells the bumblebee to fly, and it flies.

Now we remember all of that to help you get a perspective: Whatever you are dealing with, whatever you're going through, I believe God is big enough to handle it. I'm thinking that none of your troubles will be such that God will say, "This one is too hard." I don't think anything in your life is going to stump him. I don't think he will have to rub his chin and furrow his brow and say, "I've never seen this before." Wherever you are, whatever you're dealing with, God can handle it.

Deep breath. Remember.

Who Am I?

In the story of the prodigal son, we are told that while he was in the pigpen in the far country, "he came to himself." That's a weird statement, isn't it? How can *you* come to you? Did he look around one day and say, "Oh, there I am"? You know how it happens, don't you? You can get so crazy in this world, with so many people speaking into your life, that you forget who you are; you forget where you are. Just a moment ago we took time to remember who God is. Now I'd like you to take a moment to remember who you are.

Ah, you're not who the world says you are. You're not even the name you call yourself. Over and over again in the Bible, God gives people new names. You are who God says you are: beloved, chosen, redeemed, ransomed, bride of Christ, people of God, family of God, little brothers and little sisters. Children of God. Did you forget that? Remember who you are.

What Am I Doing?

Now remember what God is doing in the world. Oh, we're told that God did great and wondrous things in the world in the days of the prophets and the days of the early church, but maybe you think God doesn't work that way anymore. We're told about all the wonderful things he will do when time fades away. But God is working now—pursuing, seeking, healing, redeeming, rebuilding, and calling. God is at work now. Remember.

Remember where you are supposed to join God in his work. You may be a teacher, and there may be thirty little bright-eyed children waiting on you in the morning. Some of those kids are from broken homes. Some of them struggle to know who they are. Some of them wonder if anybody will ever love them or if they'll ever find anything they're good at. They can't color in the lines, they can't pick the right crayon, math stumps them, and their handwriting is atrocious. I know it doesn't look much like a mission field, but it's yours, isn't it?

If you could be honest with me, you'd probably use all kinds of descriptors for your office: jungle, shark tank. It would be a long time before the word *Christian* ever came up. Should it surprise you that in the middle of all of this darkness God sends you to be the light?

But Mike, you might be thinking, *there's so much darkness, and I'm just one little candle.*

It just takes one little candle, and then it's not dark anymore. I know it doesn't look like any place where God would want to do a miracle. It doesn't look like any kind of place where God would do anything special. Ah, but that's why he sent you. Everywhere, all the time, God is working in you, through you, and around you. Remember.

• • •

Forgive us, oh Father, for the times we forget who you are—when we seem to think that our mountain is the one that cannot be climbed, our ocean is the one that cannot be crossed, our problem is the one that cannot be fixed, our sin is the one that cannot be forgiven. Forgive us when we forget that with you there is no top, no bottom, no side to side. It's all you.

• • •

Forgive us when we forget who we are and act as if we are not your children, act as if we do not know you. We run from place to place begging for somebody to love us, somebody to bless us, giving away our birthright for some half-baked bowl of soup. Remind us, and help us live in the confidence of knowing who our Father is.

• • •

Give us eyes to see and ears to hear where you're at work, encouraged to jump in behind you with both feet. The details don't matter. We just want to be where you are, doing what you're doing, close enough to hear you when you laugh, close enough to hear you when you cry, close enough to help you call the lost you are seeking—that close. Don't let us ever forget. Amen.

CHAPTER ONE

A Unique Moment

$\mathcal{O}$ne recent morning I was having a cup of coffee with several of the leaders of Brentwood Baptist Church. I had been the pastor of this church for more than fifteen years, and things were going well. We were continuing to grow, several of our programs were getting national recognition, and we were meeting the budget. The conversation quickly turned to all of the changes we had witnessed over the past few years. In 2002 our church had relocated to a new campus, and with that relocation our church had experienced exponential growth. Of course, more members meant more demands on my time. My leaders, with the best of intentions, were advising me that I might be getting to the point of being overcommitted. I understood their point. We have two services on Sunday morning. (We've recently added a Sunday evening service.) We are in a building program. I teach on Wednesday night. With the usual weddings, funerals, and crisis counseling appointments thrown in, I end up with a pretty full week.

"Have you thought about giving up Kairos?" one of my leaders asked.

"No, I haven't," was my answer.

"Well, then," the other leaders offered, "perhaps you could let one of the other ministers preach for you more often."

"To be honest," I replied, "we tried rotating teachers before, and it didn't work. Besides, if you push me to give up something, I will give up Sunday morning before I give up Tuesday night."

My leaders laughed as they looked at one another. They thought I was joking. I wasn't. One of them leaned back from the table.

"Why would you rather preach on Tuesday night than on Sunday morning?"

"Think about it," I said. "The kids at Kairos get there early. They sit up front and save seats for their friends. They bring their Bibles, take notes, stay afterwards to talk about the sermon, and they e-mail me during the week with what they have learned. And if we go a little long, no one worries about it."

Who wouldn't want to teach a group that hungry for truth? Who couldn't look up and see, as Jesus said, that these are fields white with harvest? Who wouldn't want to invest their time in such a challenge?

Timing Is Everything

Kairos is the Greek word meaning "right time." New Testament Greek has two words for time. *Chronos*, from which we get our word *chronology*, means exact time like that measured by a clock. *Kairos*, on the other hand, means "appropriate time" or "fullness of time." Kairos describes the right time to tell the punch line of a joke or the right time to pick a piece of fruit from the tree. Kairos, the young adult worship experience on Tuesday night, is about creating that right moment for someone to encounter the risen Christ. Kairos is the moment Paul mentions in Romans, "For while we were still helpless, at the right time Christ died for the ungodly" (5:6 NASB). This is just the right time for the church to reach a generation with the peace, healing, and purpose promised by Jesus Christ. And like most things in my Baptist experience, it started over food.

Several years earlier I had found myself sitting in a local restaurant, surrounded by several leaders of the singles ministry at Brentwood Baptist Church. Like most churches BBC had struggled to find the right structure for our singles ministry. Because singles are mobile—that is, there is nothing to keep them from moving from one place to the next—and extremely diverse in their interests and needs, most churches find it difficult to establish and sustain an effective ministry for singles. Recently our church had been seeing some success as we structured our singles ministry around small groups. One of the small groups had developed into a relatively spiritually complex group focusing on prayer and worship. During their meetings they had begun to form a vision of a way to reach the entire young adult population. They'd started to dream about a midweek service that wouldn't be constrained by time or "church business," a ministry that would be free to speak the truth to a new generation and provide opportunities for young adults to respond to the truth they had heard in authentic worship.

This was the story I heard and the yearning I heard in the presentation several of them had put together. They had PowerPoint slides on a laptop, handouts to back up their points, and one audacious dream. These four or five members of my church wanted to start a citywide worship service for young adults.

Getting me to support it was the first step in their plan. Their presentation was impressive. They laid out the demographics. There were now thousands of young adults living in the greater Nashville metropolitan area. The proximity of several universities and colleges meant that a lot of young adults moved to the area and, due to the quality of life, ended up staying here. With growing companies in health care, banking, and, of course, entertainment, a lot of young adults were starting their lives here in middle Tennessee. Most of them were not attending church. Perhaps worse, they didn't see the need to be connected with any Christian fellowship. My young friends thought our church should do something about that.

The visionaries I was talking to were prime examples. Leigh had grown up in our church, gone off to college, and then moved home to become a rising vice president of a local public relations firm. She was confident, creative, energetic, and quickly becoming a powerful player in her organization. She was in her late twenties and spent more time in airports than she did at home. I had known Leigh and her family since I had become the pastor of Brentwood. Leigh had been a babysitter for my children. Leigh had used her personal connection to get me to the meeting.

Shaun was a major accounts manager for a large CPA firm; the others were also in significant positions in their professions. Talking with them, I understood that it would take a person of significance to get the attention of these young adults. It would require an even more significant investment to hold their attention. Each of them had full and busy lives, but the need to find an authentic expression of their faith was important enough to bring them to this meeting.

I had a few questions. Well, actually I had a lot of questions and more than a few serious doubts. First, there were already several contemporary worship services in town. Many of them were located much nearer to the places where young adults were living. Brentwood, while changing, is still a bedroom community. People move to Brentwood for the nice homes, the excellent school system, and strong community support for raising their families. Parents are involved in their children's lives; between school, soccer, music lessons, and summer camps, families are busy, even to the point of being stressed. This area is not a community where young couples buy starter homes or young adults just getting started get an apartment or their first condo. Where were all of these young adults going to come from?

I had another question: our church was a good, progressive, and growing church; but we were successful in reaching people who were in our circle of "average drive time." Churches determine the areas they are able to reach by measuring the time potential members are accustomed to driving to work, school, and shopping. Because we are a bedroom community, our average drive time is relatively short, usually about ten to fifteen minutes. There are very few young single adults in that circle of drive time. Where were all of these young people going to come from? They weren't in our church, and they weren't in our community. Suburban churches primarily focus on the ministries that engage families. Our strongest programs are aimed at preschool, children, students, and their parents. Brentwood Baptist had a singles ministry, but it was not a major focus of our church. The community simply didn't have the need.

The next problem I raised for them was a personal one for me. I didn't have time to help them. If they wanted this idea to take off, they would have to do it. I was too busy taking care of the multiple demands of a large suburban church to be involved in this start-up ministry. They agreed; in fact, they'd formed a leadership team that was already meeting. Would I help them get a place like Wilson Hall, our multipurpose facility? Would I help them choose a night and time? (We decided on Tuesday because at that time there were no good television shows on Tuesday night.) I agreed to get them started and teach a series for the first nine weeks. Then we would rotate the leadership of the services among the other teaching ministers of our staff. (This doesn't work, by the way, but it was our first plan.)

Starting Is Something

So we started. We lined up chairs in Wilson Hall, plugged in the guitars, and began to worship. Our first Kairos met on the second Tuesday night in January 2004. We started with about fifty or so in our first few weeks, but soon we were bumping over one hundred on a regular basis. The young people were having a lot of fun, and I was enjoying the teaching. But the only thing we had done was move Sunday morning to Tuesday night. Because we had guitars, we thought we were cool, but we'd kept a basic Sunday morning structure. We had not done anything to create a unique, galvanizing experience for young adults. By the end of the spring, we had peaked about 130 in attendance, finally falling back to fewer than forty in May.

It looked like this was not going to work. Yet a spark of something caught my attention. Something was going on here although we couldn't put our finger on it. Kairos had a rawness about it, an honesty that you couldn't find anywhere else. We were discouraged. We were disappointed, but no one was ready to give up. We knew this thing could work, but we were going to have to do something different.

We had planned to take the summer off so we had several months to evaluate and rethink what we were doing. At this time the leadership of Kairos wanted to go on a retreat and think through the future of Kairos. Because the retreat was planned over a weekend, I couldn't go, so the team invited Cathy Patterson. Cathy was my administrative assistant at the time, and because of my involvement in Kairos, she ended up being involved. Cathy is a people person with a lot of drive and organizational skills. If you want something done, then Cathy is the one to do it. Two important things happened when Cathy went on the retreat. First, she caught the vision of what Kairos could be. Second, she agreed to help these young adults make sure Kairos happened. (Actually, a third thing happened: I lost a good administrative assistant in the process! But the kids gained a faithful mentor and tireless leader.)

This gave the young adults someone who could work the systems of BBC. If we needed money for sound equipment or staging, Cathy could find it in someone's budget. If we needed round tables and candles, well, we suddenly found round tables and candles. Cathy can remember when we needed candles for forty tables. Surely in a church as big as ours, we could find the money for forty candles, even if they were $25 each! But we didn't have a budget, so we didn't have $25 for even one candle. Cathy led the team to sit down and ask God to provide. That night she went home and found a flyer in her mailbox from a local store, advertising the very candles at $7.88 each! It was a huge lesson for these young leaders to learn that ministry is not about human efforts. It's about trusting God.

On that first leadership retreat Cathy led the team to do a SWOT analysis of the ministry. On big posters, they listed the strengths, weaknesses, opportunities, and threats to Kairos. They sat on the back porch of the cabin they had borrowed, and they prayed over those posters. They listed the strengths; then they prayed. They listed the weaknesses; then they prayed. And so Cathy led them, wisely, to begin all over with prayer as a primary strategy.

Cathy also brought a strong accountability to the Kairos leadership. If you had agreed to do something, then Cathy became the enforcer. This allowed me to focus on the content of the teaching and the flow of the worship service while Cathy handled all of the details. For the first three years Kairos was run out of our office. Just the two of us were in charge of the fast-growing ministry. And yes, we still had to handle the regular duties assigned to the senior pastor of a growing suburban church.

That summer several key decisions were made. First, the decision was made to bring Kairos under the preaching ministry of the church. That is, the pastor's office would become responsible for the supervision and execution of Kairos. With that decision we made the statement that Kairos would be a worship service whose primary function was the proclamation of the Word. We would not be a singles ministry or a Bible study but a worship service. This sent another message to our singles and our church: we were serious. If the pastor was willing to get behind this, then Kairos must be a significant ministry.

The next decision we made was to transform Wilson Hall, a multipurpose meeting room, into more of a café destination with food, drinks, and good coffee. Instead of chairs lined into neat rows, we sat around round tables decorated with candles and studio lighting in the room and on the stage. Again we had no budget for this. But like Radar in the television series *M*A*S*H*, Cathy knew how to work the systems of BBC to get us what we needed. The leadership team prayed over every detail.

Week in and week out, God was faithful. Little by little, piece by piece, we found what we needed. Lighting, staging, sound systems, laptops, people to design Web sites, background singers, musicians, and greeters appeared as we needed them, never too soon but never too late. We were learning that God always seemed to give the manna we needed for the day.

Leadership Is Key

A few weeks later I was having breakfast with Jeromy and Jennifer Deibler, two of the founders of the contemporary Christian group FFH. Jeromy and Jennifer were members of Brentwood Baptist Church, but because they were on the road so much, we rarely saw them on Sunday morning. When they were in town for a few days, we had learned to find some time to get together. I had always loved getting together with them and hearing what was going on in their lives.

While most of us envy people of talent like Jeromy and Jennifer, I had begun to see life on the road as the grind it could be. One day over lunch, the two of them were talking about how they felt disconnected from the church. When you are gone every weekend, it's hard to feel a part of a typical congregation. Jeromy mentioned that he wished there was a way he could give back to his church. Thus began our conversation about FFH becoming the worship leaders of Kairos.

At first Jeromy wasn't too high on the idea. The last thing he wanted was to come off the road late Sunday night or early Monday morning and have to prepare a show for Tuesday. I assured him I didn't want another show. Kairos was not about a concert. Kairos was about honesty. I wanted Jeromy and Jennifer to show up and bring the worship from the place where they were. If they were down, then just be honest and worship from the shadows. If they needed to celebrate, then let us celebrate with them. Personally I had grown tired of the trend of entertainment-centered services with carefully choreographed transitions and exactly timed lighting cues. Sure, these types of services are inspiring, but they are "in the box" moments. We go, we watch, we are moved; but when we leave, we leave our worship in the box where we experienced it.

Kairos needed to offer something different. We needed to teach worship to young adults who didn't understand worship. And we had to design the service to be portable. That is, the teaching, the music, and any study aids handed out had to be usable in the hectic, everyday lives of these young adults. The worship service had to fit on an iPod or a PDA.

The last thing Kairos needed was a group of professional musicians performing for Kairos. One of the great lessons we have learned at Kairos is that there is a difference between a worship leader and a performer. Nashville has many gifted musicians of all types and genres. The running joke around Music City is that no one really works in Nashville; we just have temporary jobs while we wait on our big break. But worship leaders are harder to find. An authentic worship leader, first and foremost, has to be a committed worshipper. Worship must define their walk as followers of Christ, not be something they do in front of other people. A worship leader cannot take a congregation to a place of worship if the worship leader has never been there. (At BBC we train "lead worshippers" rather than "worship leaders".) While talent certainly helps, being a worship leader is more than just about talent. An authenticity to their presence is essential, or the congregation will not follow them into the presence of God. This is partly a spiritual gift, to be sure, but it is also a reflection of a Godward-lived life. Those who attend Kairos instinctively and quickly discern the difference. If the leader is not a person of worship, the hypocrisy is felt by the congregation, and they will not follow. So a worship leader must first be someone who worships.

A common misconception about worship leaders is that they have to be gifted musicians. This is not true. In fact, being an excellent musician can work against the effectiveness of leading worship. If the voice is too beautiful or the playing too moving, the average person in the congregation cannot sing or play at that level, so we turn into spectators and not participants. A worship leader must work to create a vertical vortex that draws people from the horizontal focus of their daily lives to the vertical focus of God's revealing himself to his people. This doesn't happen naturally but reminds us the most important task of worship leaders is to prepare themselves by worshipping and to prepare an environment that invites people to connect to Christ.

I was convinced Jeromy could be such a worship leader for Kairos. I had been to an FFH concert and watched Jeromy not only perform but also lead worship. During the invitation portion of the concert, Jeromy gave a direct, passionate, and compelling call to the gospel as well as any I have ever heard. That moment of honesty and transparency made me know he would be a gifted and fitting worship leader for Kairos. Still Jeromy wasn't convinced.

"So you don't want me to do any preparation for Kairos?"

"Nope," I answered. "I want you to spend your time preparing yourself and let your music and worship come from that."

"So what about rehearsals?" he wondered.

"That's up to you," I said. "As far as I'm concerned, you can do a sound check and go."

I didn't want them coming to Kairos with any pressure to perform. I wanted two people, serving Christ in the push and pull of the world, bringing worship from the story of their own journeys. If things were going well for FFH and Jeromy, their worship would reflect their honest joy. If things weren't going well for them, they could show us how to worship in the valleys.

I told them, "I want you to lead worship from the place where you are."

The change was dramatic, but the change wasn't in quality; it was a change in depth. In Jeromy and Jennifer and the rest of FFH, the young adults of Kairos found people who were just like them, living lives in their world, trying to keep a career and a marriage going amid the pressures of life, praising God in the context of real life.

Jeromy and Jennifer led Kairos until they accepted an invitation to go to South Africa and train other worship leaders. When they left for the six-month assignment, Michael Boggs, the lead guitarist for FFH, took over the worship leading responsibilities. Like Jeromy and Jennifer, Michael brings an honest and deep heart for worship to Kairos. People listen and respond to him because they recognize a fellow traveler who has learned to worship along the way.

I want to be sure I am clear in communicating the need for an authentic worship leader. I know Kairos is fortunate to be in Nashville where we have access to a lot of gifted musicians, but an authentic lead worshipper isn't necessarily going to be a gifted musician. The effective worship leader is going to be someone the congregation identifies with who brings their own authentic experience of worship with them. The best worship leader is the person who says, "I know where you are, I live where you live, and here are some ways to find God in the middle of the chaotic moments that make up our reality."

In Kairos you can come, lean against the back wall, sit, stand, pray, not pray, watch. How do they know this? We tell them all the time. When you come in here, it is a safe place. We take seriously the trust you show us by coming. We will do nothing to violate that trust. When we come to the worship and the prayer time, you participate in whatever way you choose. If you want to sit there with your arms folded and watch, that's fine. If you want to lift your hands in worship, if that's who you are and where you are, just keep it real. Don't lift your hands because you think that's what cool people do or because you think this makes you more spiritual than the guy sitting next to you. (It has happened when Michael is singing; someone will get up and start dancing. It has been OK as long as it didn't distract others.) We think vertical worship is good because it is directed to the Lord and is between the person and the Lord. If it's horizontal, we don't like it. We teach about the difference between vertical and horizontal worship.

When we first started Kairos, we had some big-name people come in to lead worship. They were well recognized and would sell their CDs. But the kids would not follow them. They recognized immediately that this was a horizontal show, not a vertical offering. We have had some lousy musicians who authentically loved Jesus that these kids would follow to hell and back.

A common misconception is that the leader brings the worship, that I can go find somebody who will bring worship to a congregation. That's dead wrong. You cannot conjure up worship. The individual brings it. Worship is the response of a living person to the living God. The worship leader can provide the moment. He can provide the tools, the structure to give me a good place to express my response to God, but he doesn't bring the worship into the room. This is an important thing for us to remember, particularly in settings like Kairos, because people may come in and stand in the back with their hands in their pockets. How do we measure their response? We can't put the burden on a worship leader to try something cooler next week because we don't see people participating. Manipulation is not worship. Leaving somewhere with a feeling but no change, no encounter with God, no new step of obedience is not worship. We need a worship leader who is confident enough just to worship in front of people whether they join him or not.

God Is Always Doing a New Thing

By 2005 Cathy Patterson was assuming the leadership for day-to-day details of Kairos. For almost a year she ran everything in my office and hovered over the details of setting up Kairos. When we made the decision to start using round tables to encourage conversations, Cathy put together the team that oversaw the decoration and set up of the tables every week. She put together the volunteers and made sure each team of volunteers knew their assignments.

We had greeters at the door, tech crews, and people responsible for the food and coffee setup. We had counselors prepared to talk to those who needed a friend. Volunteers ran all of it. When we took our summer break the second year, we had really led Kairos to a good place. Teaching and worship were going well, and our crowd was beginning to settle in at over three hundred.

When we started our third fall, we were in for a shock. Without any kind of warning, more than five hundred young adults showed up for our first Tuesday back from summer break! While we had done the usual bulk mailings and e-mails, we had no indication we were getting ready for that kind of jump. As we began to talk to our friends in Kairos, we found out that while the blast e-mails and direct mail pieces had been nice, the real growth of Kairos was coming from word of mouth. Young adults were telling other young adults about what was happening on Tuesday night, inviting them to "come with." Friends were bringing friends who were bringing other friends. People were getting to Kairos early, saving seats for their friends, and comparing notes afterwards.

Whether we had wanted it or not, Kairos had become a church. For one thing, numbers of people have jobs that keep them away from church on any given Sunday. Roadies for touring companies, musicians, nurses, police officers, and firefighters have to work on Sunday mornings. People in these professions were finding out about a Tuesday night service, and this was becoming their moment of worship. College kids were finding us. Finally, there was always "the friend of a friend" who wasn't attending church anywhere and found a place at Kairos, a place where they could have their honest questions honestly addressed. In our recent surveys, one third of those attending Kairos told us Kairos is the only church they attend.

What does a typical Tuesday look like? There is no typical Tuesday night. We're always mixing and matching the different elements of worship, but a standard service will always have at least three elements: musical worship, teaching, and an extended prayer time. Sometimes the worship leads to prayer that leads to teaching; other times prayer leads to worship, and that leads to teaching. And sometimes the teaching leads back to more prayer and worship. When we ask for feedback on our services, prayer is always rated as the most important time of the service. Not the teaching, not the music, but the extended time of quiet we give them for reflection, confession, and individual praise and thanksgiving.

I've been shocked to find out how many of them wanted to pray but didn't know how, and how many of them were afraid to pray because of the judgment they had felt in previous times of their Christian life. Often during Kairos I will instruct them to sit quietly and comfortably, closing their eyes. Then I will walk them through a prayer time. This way not only do they pray, but they learn a process to practice for the rest of the week. In fact, this has become an important time of teaching. As we will discuss later, many of these young adults have deep and painful issues with their fathers. As a result, addressing God as Father requires some pastoral attention. I will usually stop and remind people that Jesus was trying to give us a metaphor, a word description of how much God loves us, and that we shouldn't allow our own experience with our earthly fathers to discolor this rich portrait of God. I have to define confession and intercession; I have to define proper and improper guilt. And I do it in the few minutes of a guided prayer. You don't have to give a doctoral dissertation but a few sentences clarifying that prayer is an honest and frank dialogue between God and his children. My conversations with my own father or with my own children happen in all kinds of ways. So do our prayers. Sometimes they are quiet, sometimes they are loud, sometimes they are filled with music, and other times the weight of the pain crushes any words that would try to carry it. This is the honest experience of a believer. This is the simple, profound truth of God being with us that we try to teach at Kairos.

Since it is a worship service, we try to incorporate every facet of worship, including baptism and the Lord's Supper. One night, after a difficult and intense series on dealing with families and forgiveness (a series in which I encountered the troubling current of anger that flows in most of their lives concerning their families of origin), we observed the Lord's Supper. We'd set stations around the room, tables with the bread and cups so they could be served individually as they were ready. This night we had planned the service a little differently. In the back of the room, we had placed washtubs filled with rocks. Those in attendance were instructed to go back to the tubs and grab as many rocks as they needed to symbolize the pain, hurt, or burden they were carrying. They were to hold these rocks, and as they held each one, they were to pray for healing, for the ability to forgive, for the person who had wounded them—whatever the rock symbolized for them. They were to hold these rocks until they were through praying. Only then could they come and receive the Lord's Supper. They were to come to the table, lay down their rocks, and open their hands to receive the cup and the bread. The moments that followed stunned me. All over the room people knelt down, clutching their rocks, holding them tightly against their chests as they prayed with tears coming through clinched eyes. Slowly, one by one, in small groups, they would approach the table, carefully place their rocks on the tablecloth, and reach for the bread and cup.

What remained after the service was a sight I will never forget: the Lord's Supper table, with the used cups stacked lazily to the side, half-empty plates of bread, little purple stains of juice on the white cloth of the table—and all of it covered with rocks.

I remember kneeling down next to one of the tables and begging God to help me find a way to help these young adults find the peace of the gospel. Writing this book is part of that prayer. I am praying you will find yourself asking God to help you do whatever you have to do so these young adults can find a safe and sacred place to lay down the rocks they clutch so deeply within them.

Abba!
A Kairos Guided Prayer

Just Breathe

Just take two or three good deep breaths.

Just feel the breath come in and the air fill your lungs. Feel how alive you are in this moment, and just let go. Let go of all those things you were supposed to get done today and all you didn't get done. All the calls you were supposed to make, the things on your to-do list—none of them matter. The only thing that matters is you and your relationship with Jesus Christ. That's all. So put those other thoughts aside and let them flow away like leaves in a stream. Let them flow away . . . and just breathe.

Abba!

The first thing I want to remind you of is how much the Father loves you. Perhaps the word *Father* causes you some pain because your dad disappointed you, let you down, even hurt you. But when Jesus was asked, "What is God like?" the best picture he could find was a daddy who loves his children. Picture what it would be like to have a dad who was there for you, who gave you what you needed, who cheered for you at your ball games, who applauded at your recitals. That's the daddy that Jesus was talking about. In fact, when the disciples came to Jesus and asked him to teach them to pray, he said, "I want you to pray this way: 'Abba!'" (Luke 11:1–2, author paraphrase). This is the word for daddy, not father. It's the family word, the familiar word, the intimate word: *Dad*.

Do you realize that there has never been a time today when you've been out of his sight, out of his reach, out of his heart? There's never been a moment when he wasn't closer to you than your own breath. You may or may not have been aware of it, but that doesn't change the ultimate truth: he was there. Nothing you have done or haven't done today, nothing in your past, nothing you are afraid of—nothing has changed his mind about how much he loves you.

I'm close to my earthly dad. He and I talk about two or three times a day. He called me just this afternoon to tell me he'd be praying for me today. Whenever I head home for a visit, I know he will be standing on the porch waiting for me to get there. Can you understand God like that? When you are still enough, when you are quiet enough, when you say, "This is the moment I am going to pray," and you turn to go into the Father's presence, he's standing on the porch waiting for you to come into the house.

I'm going to give you a moment just to get there, just to feel the safety of the love, the security of his being there, knowing there is nobody or nothing big enough to take you away from him. Just get there.

How Are You?

You know what his first question is going to be? "How are you?"

Don't lie. You can't fake him out by smiling when you're hurting. You're not going to tell him something he doesn't know. He won't be shocked. Be honest. Trust him with your heart. Trust him with your reality right now. Tell him how you are. Don't worry about sounding churchy or pretty. Use the words that you know, the words that come from your gut, that come from your bones. How are you?

Do You Need Anything?

The Father's second question is "Do you need anything?"

You're tempted to be nice, to be polite, to ask for something you *should* ask. Or you're thinking, *I'll ask for something easy for God to do.* Don't.

"Is there anything too hard for God?" the prophet asked. What do you need?

- a job
- a career
- the right person

Ask. Ask from your heart, from your gut. Trust him to say yes when it is right and to say no when it is right.

Is anything wrong? Are you hurting? Have you messed up? Tell him. Own it. Tell the Father:

- This is what happened.
- This is where I was.
- This is where I failed.
- This is where I messed up and forgot who I was.

Don't try to cover it up. Just tell him.

What do you need to celebrate? What do you need to thank God for? What is going well in your life? What new treasure have you discovered? Tell him. Celebrate.

As your praise and thanksgiving come to a close, ask the Lord what he would have you to do. Much of our prayer is talking to God about what we need him to do. Let's bring our prayer time to a close by asking the Lord, "What do you need *me* to do now?"

How can the Lord use you in this moment?

- Is there a friend who is lonely, whom the Lord would ask you to contact?

- Can you be the healing one, the strong one in your family?
- Is there someone you need to forgive, somebody who needs to forgive you?
- Is there a relationship that needs to be worked out?
- Is there a call on your life to some ministry or mission?

Take a moment to listen for his answer.

• • •

Father, when we hear about how much you love us, that you'll always be there, how constant and consistent you are, it's hard for us to believe. Others have let us down, and we know how flaky we are when we make promises. But when you say, "I'll keep my promises," it's true.

• • •

I pray for my friends now. Some of them are praying simple prayers. They need your strength to get through this day, this night, this challenge. Others are praying difficult prayers—prayers that are so big and so confusing they don't see how in the world anybody, even you, can work it out. I ask, Father, that now, as they pray, they will begin to trust. I pray that your Spirit will tell them:

- *You've heard their prayers.*
- *You're already working on it.*
- *What you're working on is the absolute best they could ever have.*

• • •

For my friends who are wounded, I pray for their healing. For my friends who are angry, I pray for release and forgiveness. For my friends who are lost, I pray this will be the moment you find them. For all of us, may this be the moment that you remind us who you are and what we are in you. I pray this in your name. Amen.

CHAPTER TWO

It's More Than Starbucks

Who is the typical person who comes to Kairos? There are no typical people at Kairos. Every person arrives in God's own (*kairos*) time, in the middle of a unique journey, living a unique story. Kairos did begin as a ministry to singles by singles, but the community quickly began to expand to young married couples, college students, friends from work, and people they met around town. The downside of working with singles is that they are extremely mobile. With no family to tie them down, they are free to change churches, apartments, houses, jobs, and geography with little notice. The upside of working with singles is that they are extremely mobile. They live, work, and play all over town; and they meet a lot of people. In the course of the conversation, Kairos comes up, an invitation is offered, accepted, and one more person becomes part of the Kairos family. The only thing typical of people who come to Kairos seems to be that they want to come to Kairos.

We know some of these young adults well. They are our own young people who grew up in our church, went off to college, and have returned to the Nashville area to begin their adult lives. Others grew up in the community; their families attended other local churches, but they still feel like family to us. Of course, they bring their friends. Everyone brings their friends. Most of our growth at Kairos has come from word of mouth. The social network of the Kairos young adults is fast and effective. But there is something troubling about these young adults. Though they grew up in church, they most likely dropped out during their college years. While they were preparing for their future life, including a career, these young adults did not feel that the church had much to offer them, nothing of importance anyway. While they may be well trained in accounting, banking, legal studies, sales, computers, and medicine, they are lacking fundamental truths and life skills. Questions of identity or purpose have been put on hold. Now these young adults are stuck until they address these fundamental existential questions.

Entertained but Not Trained

Here's a troubling aspect of this reality: my own church failed them. I was the pastor of the church they grew up in, but it does not appear that we did a good job of grounding them in the basic truths of the gospel. By and large they don't study the Bible. They say no one has ever taught them how. They don't pray. Except for the desperate, "O God, help me!" prayer just isn't part of their lives. They may or may not be in a Sunday school class or small group. If they attend one, it's to hang with friends, not for the spiritual growth. Most of them are the victims of a flawed youth ministry model, the entertainment model of youth ministry. Basically we thought if we could keep the students entertained, we could keep them in the church and out of the world. There were two problems with this approach. First, no matter how many times you take your student group to the beach or the local water park, the entertainment runs dull, and the students crave additional excitement. That's why theme parks are always inventing new rides and venues. The thrill has to be constantly more thrilling, and no matter how large the budget for student ministries, the church simply can't keep up with the world when it comes to entertainment. Entertainment isn't the business of the church.

This leads us to the second problem. Because our focus was on entertaining our kids, we did not do the task entrusted to us. We did not provide them with the discipleship skills needed for a purposeful life of kingdom living. They did not learn from us basic biblical truths, basic Bible stories and characters, even basic Bible verses. They do not seriously consider the idea that a book written thousands of years ago could have anything to say to this iPod/YouTube/My Space generation. The basics of how to study a passage of Scripture and how to apply that truth to their lives were never learned. As for the deeper disciplines, such as prayer and how to discern the will of God for your life, in the shrinking world of the global economy and Internet information at your fingertips, how do prayer and seeking God fit in, much less help?

The church is not all to blame. Parents basically abdicated their roles as the primary teachers of faith to their children. Just as children were handed over to dance teachers, coaches, and music teachers, they were handed over to the student ministries of most local churches for tutorage. The children of boomers, these young adults are part of the buster generation. They have watched the way their parents lived out their faith and have, by and large, decided it was not for them. They didn't see a faith that works modeled at home. They saw materialism, divorce, and ambition dealt with in a way that was not significantly different from their secular friends' families.

Interestingly, they didn't reject Jesus. Jesus commands almost universal respect as a wise teacher and spiritual guide, but the church is seen as self-righteous and out of touch at best. At worst, the church is seen as hypocritical and bigoted. As David Kinnaman and Gabe Lyons write in their book *unChristian*, the church has an image problem. The church is no longer seen as simply being unable or unwilling to help with society's problems. The church *is* the problem. The church is seen as oppressive to minorities and close-minded to the intellectual frontiers being opened up by scientific research and development. The world is constantly changing and changing fast. The church remains static.[1]

One area of dramatic exponential change has been the development of the virtual world. Not only has the digital age increased the reach of the individual, but the digital age has also miniaturized technology to the point that a person literally has access—in some ways, control—of their entire world at their fingertips. My world, my social network, my friends, my bank, my work, my entertainment—all are available to a person with just a few keystrokes. Why can't my truth be available in the same manner? Instead of just getting the opinions of a few "dead white dudes," a young adult's worldview can be shaped by philosophies and theologies from around the world. Writers of any worldview and those who attack any worldview can be engaged on the screen in front of you.

Postmoderns have an amazing ability to hold two conflicting truths in their heads at the same time. They will tell you, "I believe Jesus is the way," and, "All religions are the same." They will say that in the same sentence. It's not a matter of logic, of its making sense. What matters is that it has to work for me right now. If next week comes and this framework no longer serves me, then I'll rework the framework.

Young adults suspect their parents didn't tell them everything there was to know. Their student minister didn't tell them everything they needed to know. They have now begun to write their own recipes for truth. It's a spiritual buffet out there. The seeker may sample any number of teachings from any number of sources. Anyone with a Web presence is considered an expert. Opinion is given equal weight to fact. Without a firm grounding in a biblical worldview, young adults are unable to distinguish the distortions from the truth they are seeking. Without ever realizing it, they drift into heretical and historical pagan teachings, thinking they have discovered something new, hidden from them by the tyrannical church.

Add to this a slowing of the maturing process, and you have a volatile mixture of false teaching, immaturity, and resources.

Homeless with No Name

Young adults today find themselves in a crisis. They are starting their adult lives. They are on their own. They have graduated college, found a job, and may have moved away from home for the first time. Now they can do anything they want, and some of them do. They are caught between childhood and adulthood. They want to play Wii games with their friends until 2:00 a.m., but now they have to be at work at 8:30. They are pushed to compete in an ever more competitive job market that leaves them little time for social interaction or connection. Sure, they text one another or leave messages on their Facebook pages, but they still feel lonely for long periods of time. They want to go places and do things, but they only have so much money. They try the club scene, but it soon grows boring. They want to meet someone special, but how? And when you find that someone special, what do you do next? In this area they are particularly unequipped.

This generation is emotionally and relationally handicapped because, for the most part, they are the products of divorce. Most of the young adults we deal with at Kairos have watched their parents divorce. They're dealing with the challenge of blended families. Most of the young adult men do not have a positive male role model in their lives. Fewer and fewer children have the security and emotional safety of growing up in a home where parents love each other. If the parents are still together, the relationship is strained. Every year I talk to a smaller and smaller percentage of young adults who grew up in a loving, two-parent home. I know you may think I am exaggerating, and your experience may be different. I am reporting what I have discovered every Tuesday night for the last four years.

I see young men trying to be husbands who've never seen a husband modeled in their homes. They're trying to be fathers, and they had no father. Young women are trying to be wives and mothers, and they have no pattern to follow. Most of our education in how to function as adults does not come from formal training but from the informal observations of watching our parents live their lives. What happens when there are no healthy models to watch?

You watch television. You go to the movies. You read magazines and create a mental collage of what a father looks like, what a family looks like, a wife, a mother; and all of these pictures are based on varying degrees of reality. It's no wonder so many of these young adults are unhappy in their relationships or unable to sustain a relationship at all.

There are gaping holes in the souls of these young adults, particularly in the areas of self-identification and self-worth. They don't know who they are; therefore, they do not know how much they are worth as persons. During a child's life there are several important moments when a parent, grandparent, or significant adult speaks a "you are" phrase to the child. The adult will say, "You are smart," or, "You are pretty," and that statement becomes part of that child's identity. Like some ancient naming ritual, the words that follow the "you are" statement mark the child for life. Of course, negative comments following the "you are" statements are carried with children for the rest of their lives as well. These life-killing statements take a painful toll on children as they grow into young adulthood.

If, however, the significant adult is absent for any reason and the "you are" statement goes unspoken, children begin a quest to find out who they are. The last place these children will look is within, so they begin a journey to find an outside figure to validate their identity. The media is filled with all kinds of messages to a young adult on this quest, but instead of "you are" statements, our culture sends "you are not" statements. The magazines tell our young women they are not thin enough, not pretty enough, not sensuous enough. The epidemic of eating disorders is just one of the tragic consequences of a young adult looking for a "you are" validation, only to hear, "You are not."

Young men are looking for "you are" statements as well; they hear, "You are not" in many ways throughout our culture. Currently we are dealing with a steroid scandal in professional sports. Professional athletes at the top of their respective games take steroids to enhance their performance because they are afraid of being told, "You are not strong enough, fast enough." Our young men are told they don't make enough money; they don't wear the right clothes, drive the right car, or know the right people. While every generation has dealt with peer pressure, the difference with generation X or the busters is that there is not a family or community around the child to combat the negative messages of the culture. Most of us have had a moment when we were told something cruel by our classmates only to have a parent, grandparent, or significant adult tell us, "That's not true, child, you are . . ." Without trustworthy "you are" statements, young adults are trapped in an endless cycle of trying on as many identities as they can find, hoping they will find one that fits.

The gospel is filled with "you are" statements. You are chosen, beloved, called, redeemed. I could go on and on. Yet many people assume, with some justification, that if they come to church, the only message they're going to hear is, "You are not." You are not "doing enough for God." You are not "good enough." Many young adults think that going to church will not only not help them but will actually do them more harm. In their minds the church has become another voice of judgment and condemnation, a constant and painful reminder of all of the ways they fall short.

This brings many young adults to a point of crisis. They are now making their own decisions, but they're trying to do it without a strong-centered core of identity. This process of trying to find one's identity by trial and error usually ends up being painfully disappointing. Lifestyle choices are made not from any clear understanding of right and wrong, not from a moral compass, but simply because a friend recommended a certain course of action or something in the media caught their attention. Rarely do they begin with the understanding that they are unique individuals, created in the image of God and of unspeakable value, because no one has ever told them this basic truth about themselves. They begin by assuming there is something lacking within them, and they go out to find something in the world to fill the void.

One night at Kairos I told the story of watching *Antiques Roadshow*. This television show is about a group of antique experts and appraisers who travel around the country, telling people what their stuff is worth. Average Joe brings his family heirlooms, paintings, or pieces of furniture for appraisal, and it's always interesting to hear the expert tell the owner about the piece set in front of him. Inevitably someone brings something their family has told them was extremely valuable, only to find out it's a cheap imitation worth a few bucks. The highlight of the show is when someone brings an object and has no idea that it is extremely valuable.

"Where did you get this?" the expert will gasp, pulling on his white gloves. (When the white gloves come out, you know the show is about to get serious.)

"My grandmother gave it to me," Average Joe will reply.

"And what do you do with it?" the expert inquires.

"Oh," says Joe, "I keep my change in it."

You can see the expert grab the table to steady himself.

"You do what?" he sputters, more an accusation than a question. "Do you know what this is?"

Of course the owner has no idea, giving the expert an opening to launch into a detailed history of the object, how there are only three of them in the world.

"See," the expert will say reverently turning the object over, tracing the name of the artist. "See where it's signed. This is the signature of the great master."

"How much is it worth?" Average Joe now wants to know.

"I have no way of telling you," the expert replies. "It's too valuable ever to put a price on. It's priceless."

I told the Kairos gang that I wished there were some way I could walk out and grab them one by one, turn them upside down, point to God's signature, and say, "See! This is where God himself signed you! That's the signature of the greatest artist of all time. His signature across your life makes you too valuable ever to put a price on. That's what we mean when we say you are created in the image of God. You are priceless."

After Kairos that night a young lady waited to talk to me. By the time she got to the little café table where I was sitting, she was crying so hard her thin shoulders heaved. After several minutes she was able to get her breath.

"I didn't know that," she sobbed. "I didn't know God had signed me. Nobody told me that. Things would be different if I had known that."

She looked up at me after a long pause.

"I would be different if I had known that."

This is who comes to Kairos. They will come to Kairos long before they would ever think about coming to church. The interesting thing is that we do not have to convince these young people that they need God. We don't need to make the case for God. They are seekers. They know they want something. That's why they've taken the extraordinary step of setting foot in a church on a Tuesday night. By walking in, they are saying, "I'm open to something. I need or want something."

I've thought about which people in the Gospels might come to Kairos. The Samaritan woman would come, and she'd be back with friends. Peter, loudmouthed and trying to get it together, would come. He'd be the first to leap into a mission project. John would come and would have a table of friends because he values community. Thomas would come and stay afterward to ask questions. Nicodemus would come, but he would not be seen. He'd slip in the back after the music had started, lean against the wall in the darkness, and leave right before things ended. He'd e-mail me later.

First and foremost, those who come are looking for a safe place, and we go to great lengths to make sure Kairos is a safe place. We make sure they know we like them, which is different from love. Everybody knows Christians are supposed to love. But what Christians don't do well is like people. We take seriously the trust that is placed in us by those who attend Kairos. We know it's as close to church as some of them will get. It may be weeks or months before they let us know they've been attending. It's not unusual at all for me to be somewhere in the community, and young adults will come over to talk to me about Kairos. In the course of the conversation, they will confess to me that they haven't yet filled out an attendance card or even let us know their e-mail address. Trust is a big issue with these young adults. It is difficult to get and easy to lose.

Cautious but Curious

People who come to Kairos want to be engaged in the process, but they want to control the process, to take next steps whenever they are ready to take them. They're not going to follow a prescribed path or timetable. We've learned to wait until one of them initiates the conversation, letting the process flow from there. The starting point may be something we are doing in missions, something they saw on television, a life skills question. More times than not, the question is about me or our church. The first thing they want to know is whether they can trust us. Two things prompt this cautious approach. First, they've been let down by authority figures and significant adults. An effective leader of young adults is going to have to possess a comfortable self-awareness. The conversation usually begins with why we started Kairos and how I got involved. They will want to know about my own conversion and the details of why I am in the ministry. They will even ask some questions about my marriage. The trustworthiness of the leadership of Kairos is a major issue for those who attend. They don't expect us to know everything, but they do expect us to be honest about what we know and what we don't.

Second, they've seen through the veneer of the established church; they do not readily accept the church or the Bible as authoritative or genuine. If we can pass their initial tests and earn their trust, then they will start their journey toward faith. Now, mind you, this journey rarely looks like the conversion of Paul on the road to Damascus. Nicodemus would be a better model—lots and lots of questions from a distance, then a slow advance toward belief. They want to know some answers, and they want to wrestle with the implications of these answers themselves. Don't expect them to believe something just because you say it or just because the Bible says it. This generation is familiar with several sacred texts; the Bible is one of them, but just one of them. If the Bible is to be trusted, then like everything else it has to be tested.

One way to test it is to watch Christians work. Kairos attendees are excited about and interested in missions. They are not that excited necessarily about evangelistic mission efforts; but building houses, painting schools, working with the poor, medical mission efforts—anything where they can see Christians work in a way that makes a real and practical difference in the lives of someone else engages them. When I first started as a minister, the message came before the ministry. Now the ministry comes before the message. That is, people have to see the love of Christ in action before they will take your witness seriously.

This was one of the first real predicaments we faced at Kairos. We were planning a trip to New York to paint some inner-city schools when we realized that a few of those who had signed up were not Christians. We had never thought about sending non-Christians on a mission trip. To be honest, the question simply hadn't come up. After all, why would a non-Christian want to go on a Christian mission trip, especially when we communicated that the purpose of the trip was to show the love of Christ in a real and tangible way? But for the young adults in question, painting the school was a worthy cause, something they could believe in. They wanted to go. So, after several prayerful meetings, the leadership team decided to let people who were not yet Christians participate in the missions trip with the prayerful hope this might allow us to engage them in a more serious conversation about their faith. I don't know if I would do this every time, but this time it did work. Two professions of faith followed the mission trip.

This brings up another change in the way we do ministry. In previous years becoming a Christian meant joining the church. Not anymore. Just because young adults become followers of Jesus, just because they are baptized, it doesn't follow that they are going to want to be members of a church. That is an entirely different step, one that will take just as long to make. These young adults love keeping their options open. Once they decide to follow Jesus, they will fill their discipleship plate from the buffet of American religious life. It's not unusual for an individual to be participating in two or three churches at the same time. They may worship at one church, participate in a small group at another, and get involved in a ministry project at yet another. Those of us who lead local churches wonder how we can make this work in the long run. Almost daily I am reminded that few of these young adults are interested in helping the established church work. For them it is all about "my journey," what helps me get to where I need to be. One of the challenges facing organized religion in the future is the question of how we are going to adapt to the changing understanding of what it means to be a member of the church and a follower of Christ.

Young adults view the contemporary religious landscape like the story of the three blind men who encountered an elephant. One man grabbed the tail and said, "The elephant is like a rope." The other placed his hand on the side of the elephant and said, "The elephant is like a wall." The last man grabbed the elephant's leg and said, "The elephant is like a tree." Each man had the truth but only part of the reality of the elephant. God is so vast, so mysterious, that no one person or group can capture all of him. These young adults accept that congregations, like the blind men, will grasp some part of the ultimate reality of God but not all of him. They will go to whatever church specializes in the part they need to experience. Experience is important to postmoderns.

N. T. Wright says, "Postmodernity is the necessary judgment against the arrogance of modernity."[2] Modernity says life is a science. We can fix it. We can figure it out. If there is something wrong, we can do the medicine, the math, the chemistry. We can make a body part better than the original body part: knee, shoulder, whatever. Knowledge is power. Modernity is about getting education and more education, more studies, more research. Modernity prizes information.

We are bombarded with information. I can be literally anywhere in the world with a couple of clicks on the keyboard. I can find a camera that will show me what is happening in downtown Delhi, then click again and see the ocean breaking on the shores of Cape Town, South Africa. I can find news faster than it happens. I can watch the plane crash into the World Trade Center. There is always breaking news. There is instant messaging, cell phone texting, blogging, Facebook. All of this brings a sense of knowing but not a real knowing. A sense of community, but only virtual community. We have ended up with a modern-day Tower of Babel.

Young adults are rediscovering the mystery and transcendence of God. The modern emphasis on rationality and the logical expression of the gospel has frustrated them. From their experience life doesn't always make sense or follow a formula. Nothing adds up the way it is supposed to. It follows then that they do not want a God who can be captured in logical syllogisms and rational arguments. This God must be encountered to be known. He cannot be contained or captured, and they are suspicious of anyone or any system that claims to have God in a box.

Yes, doing church like this is messy. The conversations are dynamic and spontaneous but rarely linear. You rarely go from point one to point two, following all of the subpoints along the way. The teachable moments in their lives erupt, and they are intercepted in text messages and e-mails—digital flares sent up from a life lived on the move. If you are going to work with these young adults, you are going to have to move with them. They don't care that you don't have all of the answers. They're looking for an honest friend who will stay with them on the journey.

What's Your Name?
A Kairos Guided Prayer

Let Go

Just close your eyes and put both feet on the floor. Get comfortable. Begin by taking just a few deep breaths. Take a break from the day and allow what you had to do today to stay in today. As you anticipate tomorrow, just let it stay in tomorrow. It will be there when you get there. There are no elves showing up at your workplace doing your work. That stack you left on your desk will still be there. So just be here, right now, in this moment, in this place.

What's Your Name?

I'm going to ask you an obvious question. I want you to hang with me. Do you know your name? I'm not talking about the name your parents gave you. I'm talking about the name you gave yourself. When you talk to yourself, how do you talk to yourself? What is the name you call yourself? Sometimes it's slang, like "kid," "little girl," "girlfriend," "big man," or something like that. Sometimes it's hurtful, isn't it? Sometimes it's "stupid" or "idiot" or any other number of words I could add that we can't say in polite company. You would never speak to anyone else that way, but it's the name you call yourself.

I don't want to bring up any deep pain or cause you any pain, but I want you to hold onto that name just for a second. Where did that name come from? Was it a mistake? Was it something you thought you should have done well but was a failure instead?

In that moment of weakness, in that moment of loss, in that moment of defeat, did you name yourself? Did someone else name you? Did someone call you a "loser"? Did someone call you a "screwup," and you took that name to be your own?

What's Your New Name?

It's interesting. Anytime anyone met Jesus, there was a name change. Saul became Paul; Simon became Peter. When did your name change? Do you know the moment when you met Jesus? You may not know the exact day, the exact time. As I explain to people, when I gave my life to Christ, I wasn't looking at my watch. I don't know the time, but I know when it happened. Did your name change? Did your identity change? The apostle Paul said, "If anyone be in Christ he is a new creation. The old has passed away" (2 Cor. 5:17, author paraphrase).

To the church of Pergamum, one of the seven churches in Revelation, Jesus said, "I will give you a name written on a white stone. The name is known only to you and to me" (Rev. 2:17, author paraphrase). It was the promise of Jesus to a persecuted church: "I know your name."

So tell me now, what is the name Jesus gave to you? Who are you? Not, "What did your parents name you?" Not, "What name did you give yourself?" I want to know the name Jesus gave you. Do you know who you are? Do you know whose you are? It's vital that you know this. If you don't, the world will name you. The world will define you. Know the name that Jesus gave you.

●   ●   ●

Lord Jesus, in this moment of quiet and stillness, we ask honestly, "Who am I? Tell me my name." Name us. Name us in a way that reminds us even in this moment that we are part of your family. And we pray this in your name. Amen.

CHAPTER THREE

The Unseen Damage of Cultural Christianity

hen I was a student in seminary, we were required to spend an evening doing a "ride along" with the local police. I was assigned to an officer in the most crime-riddled part of town. I was to ride with him from 3:00 p.m. to 11:00 p.m. in order to get a little exposure to life in the inner city. Growing up white, suburban, and middle-class did not prepare me for what I was to experience that night. The officer I rode with was a nice enough guy, but he was a guy who had seen too much and had little time for the fluff of life. Carrying around a seminary student was not exactly the way he had wanted to spend the evening. After signing a waiver that said I understood I could be in harm's way and would not sue the city if I got shot (*shot?*), we got in the car and started our rounds.

He drove by memory, rarely paying attention to the official street markings. He drove with a speed and assurance that told me he was confident he knew how every street twisted and turned, knew just what he could expect as he made each turn. He checked on several senior adults in the projects. He drove by several places first, just to see if anything was going to be happening there that night. I was surprised by how well he knew most of the people on the street. He called them by name. They would walk over to the car, lean down, and exchange some kind of banter with the officer. He'd arrested a lot of these people; he'd probably have to arrest some of them again. It was the cat and mouse game they played downtown.

Things were pretty quiet until about 9:30 p.m. when we responded to the scene of a knife fight. When the radio call came in, he flipped on his lights and sirens and did a 180-degree turnaround in the middle of the street, rolling his cruiser up on the sidewalk to complete the turn. He cussed under his breath and muttered something about working overtime tonight. We turned into an alley and met up with another officer as we waited for the ambulance to pick up the victim and transport him to the hospital. The officers walked around canvassing the people who were standing around the scene. They found out the name of the man who had committed the crime. The officer I was riding with knew him. We hopped in the car and began to look for our suspect at the places he was known to hang out. We found him at his girlfriend's house. After a minor altercation, he was arrested, handcuffed, and placed in the back of our cruiser. We took the suspect to the precinct to begin the booking process. While filling out one of the reports, the officer had to get up and go into another room for some more forms.

He left me alone in the room with the suspect. I knew he was handcuffed, but that gave me little comfort.

"What are you doing here?" he asked me. Before I could answer, he began to guess.

"You with the DA?"

"No," I said.

"Detective?"

"No."

Finally, when he ran out of guesses, I explained that I was a seminary student assigned to ride along with the officer.

"Are you gonna be a preacher?" he asked.

"Yes, I am."

"What kind?"

"Baptist."

He let out a stream of curse words.

"What about that?" he laughed. "I'm a Baptist."

There I sat with a man who had just pulled a knife on another man, slicing across his stomach from hip bone to hip bone, and now he was proudly telling me that he was a Baptist. Apparently what he said he believed didn't impact many of the choices he made.

Setting Examples

The young adults in Kairos grew up in such homes. Many of them were taken to church by their parents. The parents may have attended church with them or more likely dropped them off at the nearest church because the parents believed religious instruction was important to their child's moral development. There may have been a Bible in the home. Yet for all of the trappings of a Christian home, there was nothing distinctly Christlike in their homes. Daily decisions were made using the same criteria everyone else used: Will this advance my career? Is the home nicer? Are the schools better? Will they help my child get into a better college? Christianity and church were important because they reinforced the characteristics required for chasing the American dream. For most of the young adults of Kairos, church was part of the middle-class ethic they grew up with. It may or may not have had anything to do with Christ, but they learned that this was Christianity; they perceived this was what it meant to be a Christian.

For the vast majority of my professional career in the church, success has been about attendance. We measured the success of our church and the success of our ministers by how many people we could get to attend an event. Churches were gauged according to their average attendances of worship and Bible study. Of course, all of us wanted to be successful, so we learned to focus on attendance.

We developed any number of schemes and programs to encourage attendance. Church growth was measured by baptisms, the number of people who had made professions of faith in a given year. Year after year, we worked our programs to increase attendance and baptisms. Tragically, we did not put the same emphasis on growing believers into maturity.

Thus faith was perceived as something that was emotional and momentary. People would gather together and worship, experience a rush of joy, then go out to live their lives in the real world, just trying to hang on until next Sunday. My Sunday experience and my faith were segregated from the rest of my life. There was church, and there was the world; the two never intersected. I might come to church, worship and study as a committed believer. Outside the walls of the church, we worked and lived in a world governed by the rules of unbelievers. There was never an expectation that what was talked about on Sunday would have anything to do with what was going on in my life on Monday. I am pushing this point to an extreme, but the reality is that most busters grew up in homes where Christianity was a thin veneer painted on the surface of carnal lives.

Because we had little expectation of spiritual formation and because there was almost no accountability in the disciple's walk toward maturity, only a few chosen saints managed to grow in their faith. Most of us remained shallow in our walk with Jesus, and most of the time being in shallow water seems fine. But if life turns stormy, the shallow water is the most dangerous place to be.

Drawing Conclusions

In watching their parents, these young adults came to their first conclusion: Christianity doesn't mean much. In everyday decisions, in everyday behaviors and choices, faith doesn't have significant influence. Their houses were pretty much like other houses. Jobs and career choices, entertainment choices, the clothes they wore, how the money was spent—these decisions were made in a manner pretty much like everyone else. The pressure of the socioeconomic strata of the family went much further in determining the values of the family than any overarching Christian worldview. This disconnect of faith from real life continued in raising the children. In conversations between parents and children, the focus was rarely on the child's life being lived with a kingdom purpose. The parents were more focused on getting good grades, getting ahead socially, getting the child into a good college and launched into a successful future. Add to this the "enlightened" view taken by most of the boomer parents. Children were allowed to find their own way to faith. Parents did not want to impose their religious beliefs on their children. For a lot of the late sixties, seventies, and into the eighties, parents decided that their children would have to figure out religion for themselves. The children decided if and when they would go to church and what they would believe about God, if they chose to believe at all. Message: Christianity is nice but not necessary.

The second thing young adults concluded was that Jesus is not real. At least, Jesus is not real in any way that can empower people in living their lives. Jesus is recognized as a great teacher, a smart man who gives wise counsel, but this counsel is only a suggestion. The teachings of Jesus are not authoritative. They were spoken several thousand years before computers and PDAs, Internet and HD television. Jesus may have had good stuff for another time, but the centuries have taken some of the edge off his teachings. Jesus, Buddha, and Mohammad probably had some insight into the truth, but Jesus probably didn't have it all. How could he? Look at everything we have discovered since he lived.

Popular culture no longer encourages faith. At the least, the world is amused by it; at worst, open hostility is growing daily—the postmodern insistence that there be no absolute truth, the sciences demanding every aspect of life submit to the scientific method. While these factors may not kill faith in our children, they do wither any budding belief. Getting through high school and college, much less graduate degrees, without having your faith openly challenged or attacked takes some doing. The result is a loss of confidence on a grand scale. Young adults no longer trust what they have been taught in church or what others have said about their faith. How much can we trust what we know about Jesus? Some scholars insist that we have few actual words of Jesus in the Bible, that most of what is assigned to Jesus was actually said about him in the early church and later written as if Jesus had said it. Young adults approach the beginning of their adult lives—new job, new city, and all of the choices and responsibilities such a moment brings—and by now they have relegated Jesus to the back part of their brain where they keep the rest of the childhood memories. Jesus is nice but really not helpful, like a gift from your grandmother. You smile and say thank you when you get it, but you know you will never really wear it.

In addition, and it pains me to say this, we have done such a lousy job teaching the faith in most churches. How can the study of Jesus be boring? In the words of Dallas Willard, "Jesus is at least the smartest man ever to live."[3] How then can we put someone in a room with a Bible for an hour a week and have them walk out thinking Jesus is boring? I don't know, but that is what we have done. Mention Sunday school to young adults, and if they don't laugh out loud, they will at least scrunch up their face as if they had just bitten into some bad-tasting food.

Of course, the whipped cream on top of this anxiety sundae is the public face of Christianity for most young adults. Since most of them didn't attend church while they were in college, they watched television; in particular, they watched televangelists. The money-focused prosperity gospel and the front-page stories of ministers behaving badly have sapped whatever confidence these young adults had in institutional Christianity. They had no spiritual foundation, no personal relationship with Christ. As a result, they became a target for anything that came down the road. Many of them will tell you they believe this or that, but it has no real place of authority in their lives. If they want to do something else, they will change their entire theological framework to support what they want to do.

We call this a worldview. A worldview is a philosophical framework from which all of life's decisions are made. The young adults we have met, by and large, almost totally lack a Christian worldview. Their worldview is made up of a hodgepodge of experiences. Moments from movies, lyrics from favorite songs, quotes from books and magazines are pasted together in a collage entitled "How I See the World." Interestingly, many of the items that make up the worldview of these young adults are contradictory, if not mutually exclusive. The incongruent worldview leads to incongruent lives and decisions. Sometimes, when you talk to these young adults, they will answer your questions with totally conflicting responses. One response comes from one part of their worldview and another answer comes from another part. They may not even recognize the discrepancy, even when you point it out. What they think about sex is a prime example. In their world sex is everywhere. Entertainment, advertising, and most of their song lyrics talk about expressing one's sexuality. So they will engage in sexual relations, saying that the behavior "doesn't really mean anything," then be surprised by the emotional impact of the act. They are, in the words of the New Testament, double-minded people and rudderless ships tossed to and fro by every wind of doctrine.

Correcting Perceptions

As you can imagine, this leads to a life crisis for these young adults. They are on their own, starting to build the life they have always dreamed about. They leave home, get a job, and now . . . Well, that's the hard part. Now what? What is right? What is wrong? How do I know? Is there a plan? What am I supposed to do? Where are my friends? Who will be my family? Many have only negative images, memories from their past that they reject. While they may not know what kind of father or husband they should be, they know what kind of father or husband they don't want to be. They may not know what kind of mother or wife they want to be, but they know what kind they don't want to be. So what if their parents were successful professionals who made lots of money? So what if they had the boat, the lake house, the condo at the beach? They were always tired, always sucked dry, always behind, always frustrated, rarely happy. Their marriages fell apart. They missed significant events like ball games and ballet recitals. They didn't have time to talk to their children, didn't spend time with their children. Their children had everything yet felt abandoned. Abandonment is a huge issue for this generation. So the young adult knows only, "I don't want to live like that." The problem is you can't live *against*. You have to live for. But most of them don't know what this "for" is. So they start looking for something to help them make sense of their lives.

They look around for people who appear to have their life together, and they look for people who will love them. One of the most important things we do at Kairos is show up. Every Tuesday they understand that Kairos will be there. When we first started Kairos, we only met during the school year. We would take a break at the beginning of June and start back with the beginning of local schools in mid to late August. At the first summer break we took, the attendees at Kairos were frustrated. "Where are we going to go?" they asked us.

To be honest, we leaders needed the break, but the more we talked to those who attended Kairos, the more we were convinced that Kairos would soon have to become a year-round ministry. We didn't set out to start another church, and technically Kairos is not a church but a closely connected ministry of Brentwood Baptist Church. After all, I am the senior pastor at Brentwood and the primary teacher at Kairos. All of our staff is also on staff at Brentwood Baptist Church, so we are not a freestanding church. But we carry out the functions of a church. We teach the Word, we share the Lord's Supper and baptism, we have fellowship and respond when pastoral care is needed—all things any church would do. But we have come to realize that one of the most important things we do is to be there, to be consistent and authentic. Kairos is both their church and their home.

I have come to realize that I am not only their teacher, but I am a father figure. I have to work to make up for the absent authorities in their childhood, for the untrustworthy guardians who disappointed them or left them unprepared for adulthood. One of the biggest requirements is that I be authentic. I've learned that I don't have to be perfect, but I do have to be real. Primarily, I have to be real about who I am as a leader. My faith walk has to be evidenced for all to see. And they will test their leaders. Do you read the Bible? When? For how long? What difference does it make? Do you pray? When? Does Jesus answer? How do you know? Are you married? Do you love your wife? How can we know? If I call you, will you be there? What if I tell you my secrets, secrets no one else knows? Will you keep my trust? Will you still be there for me? Will you keep your promises?

The questions are that pointed and that personal. I usually work out on Tuesday afternoon, and I take my wedding ring off while I work out because the weights scratch my ring. One Tuesday, in my rush, I hadn't put my ring back on and showed up at Kairos without it. Afterwards, several of the young men walked up to me and wanted to know where my ring was. That was one of my first clues as to how closely they were watching my life. It also reminded me how important my marriage is to those who attend Kairos. They like seeing my wife Jeannie when she can come. They like to know that I buy her flowers every time I go to the grocery store; that the checkout clerks ask me, "How did you screw up this time?" They like hearing stories about my life, how I overcame an obstacle or how I should have done better. Not that the teachings are about me; they are not. But remember, most of these young adults have never seen an authority figure live out the faith in front of them.

You have to be willing to live out your life in front of them in order to be heard by them. That's why we've found it imperative to have consistent leadership in our worship and teaching. Week in and week out, we have the same worship leaders and the same teachers. There are always people on the platform who are recognized by the attendees of Kairos. If I have to be out and we have a guest speaker, then the worship leadership is the same. If the worship leader is on the road, then I am there. Cathy Patterson, director of Kairos, works the room, manages all the details that say, "Welcome," calls them by name. The counselors who stand in the back are familiar faces. Yes, this is a big commitment to make. You need to consider this from the first meeting on. You have to be there. This age group is slow to trust and quick to assume you are like everyone else. There is a price to be paid for the right to be heard by them. You have to make up for a lot of disappointment in their lives.

It's quite a responsibility, the authority they give me. It's a little spooky sometimes. We were in the middle of a series on relationships once, and I had the women stand up.

"Guys," I said, "the word *pastor* means 'father.' That's where it comes from. All these ladies you see, all of them, are my daughters, and I take that responsibility seriously. Now, if you have anything other than Christ's best in mind for them, I have one word for you: good-bye. And if you don't think I'll call the Brentwood Police on you, you're nuts."

Then I had the guys stand up.

"Ladies," I said, "these are princes in the kingdom. They are in training for a significant role in what God is doing in this world. If you are not part of helping them become the rulers God wants them to be, I have a word for you: good-bye."

You have to be willing to lay it on the line for them. You have to be willing to share your story and listen to theirs. You have to drink a lot of coffee and read a lot of e-mails, most of which begin with "I don't know why I am writing you, but . . ." Slowly, one young adult at a time, you will begin to gain their trust as they begin to tell one another that you are for real. Then you can speak into their lives, and they will give you permission to say what you need to say. If it's confrontational, they expect you to hold them accountable to the promises they have made to Christ and to one another. If it's encouragement, the encouragement has to be rooted in reality. You can't just blow smoke at them.

In our culture we are so concerned about self-esteem that we no longer tell our children or one another the truth. We cut off honest dialogue with empty platitudes about being able "to do anything you want." That's not truth. A commercial on television tells me if I buy a pair of Michael Jordan's basketball shoes, I can "be like Mike." No, I can't. If I buy those shoes, I will still be the slow, fat, white guy in the middle of the court. The only difference is that I will be wearing two-hundred-dollar shoes. The encouragement you bring has to be rooted in who they are as persons. Their gifts and passions, their life experiences, their dreams and abilities—all are useful clues to help them discover God's purposes for their lives. One of the best things that happens in Kairos is being there long enough to see some of them grow into the persons Christ created them to be and to see how he redeems past mistakes and wounds to make them even stronger in the service of his kingdom.

Too many people see the church as a place of bigotry and close-mindedness. There are more examples of the body of Christ failing to live out his teachings of love for our neighbor than we need for the next hundred years. The perceived bigotry of the local church has been rebutted by a cultural teaching of tolerance. According to the teaching of tolerance, we have to accept any behavior on anyone's part as long as it doesn't hurt anyone. What constitutes harm to another is a matter of intense debate. But to be tolerant, you can say anything about the choices of another. All truth claims must be respected, no matter how internally inconsistent they may be. Young adults are looking for someone to help them find the truth—a truth they can live in the real world, their world. This isn't your father's Oldsmobile, and it's certainly not your father's world. Things are changing too fast and have transformed everything we do. When I began my ministry, we would write letters, letters that took days to process by mail. Now I am expected to get an e-mail or text message instantly and respond just as fast. Young adults are looking for a faith, a reliable truth that can help them make sense out of an unpredictable world. They are looking for people who are sure of this truth, sure enough to stake their lives on it, sure enough to speak it boldly.

Actually, this hasn't changed much from the early church. In their letters to the early church, Peter and Paul told the first Christians to live out their faith in front of their cities so that everyone could see the power of the gospel. From the beginning the greatest testimony to the power and reality of the living Christ has been the changed lives of his believers. Now, as then, we are in a time when there are so many truth claims, so many enemies of the faith, the truth of Christ has to be lived out in front of them before it is heard. That's the challenge of leading a Kairos crowd. You have to be the message you want to preach.

The World Revolves:
A Kairos Guided Prayer

Exhale

I don't know what kind of day you've had. I don't know if it's been a good week for you or a bad one. Is it one of those weeks when every day is Monday? It doesn't matter. I know sometimes we get excited and hung up, thinking that everything revolves around how we are doing in the moment. It's a good day if we get a few breaks, if we can find the right parking spot or hit traffic right.

So breathe out. Take all that pressure off yourself. The universe doesn't depend on what you and I are doing at the moment. The sun came up this morning and didn't ask your permission. It went down in the evening and didn't check with you. The stars held their place, the earth spun in its orbit, and you didn't have a thing to do with that. The seasons change, the world tips on its axis, the cycles of life continue. It's not up to you. The ultimate reality is based on this one unchanging truth: Jesus Christ is Lord. That doesn't change if it rains; that doesn't change if it's hot; that doesn't change if you're up or if you're down.

He's Lord of the heights, Lord of the depths, Lord of the wide spaces and the narrow places. He's Lord as far as you can see and as deep as you can go. There's no place, nowhere that he is not Lord. And with that understanding we his people can relax and focus on the mission that he has given to us. We can concentrate on the relationship we have with him, knowing that no matter what the world throws at us, he's strong enough to work it out for his glory, for his kingdom, so that in the end of it all we will thank him for every moment. We will look back and see how he worked in those moments when we swore, "This is the worst thing that could ever happen." We'll see how he worked and used it. And we'll stand in front of him and say, "We wouldn't change a thing. I wouldn't give you that moment back because of what I learned on the journey."

In that confidence take a deep breath. Close your eyes; get comfortable. As I lead you through this time of prayer, I promise you: you are safe here. No one is walking around. No one is looking at you. We aren't going to sneak up on you and baptize you while you're not looking. You are free to participate in any way you need to. If you want to raise your hands in praise and thanksgiving, feel free to do that. If you want to hold your head in your hands, you do that. Whatever this moment is for you, it's OK. Just keep it as real as you can. Don't worry about what anyone around you is doing. This is just you. Just breathe.

God Loves You

I know that for most of you, it is hard to understand how the Father delights in you, how much he loves you and how he longs to be with you. You haven't had that from anybody else in the world, and it's hard for you to grasp that this great God, Creator of heaven and Earth would want to spend any time with you. I don't just say that because I'm a pastor and it's my job to say it. I say it because it is my own testimony, my own witness to you. I say it on the testimony of thousands of saints I have known and the millions across the generations who have testified in books and in journals and in scratchings on the walls of catacombs about the love of the Father who will not let you go. I say it based on thousands of years of witness from men and women like Abraham and Sarah, Hannah, Gideon, David, Rebecca, Jacob, Peter, John Mark, the apostle Paul, Mary, Mary Magdalene—all who were found and loved by God.

Across time and space, across the heavens, the love of the Father has sought after you. This love that will not take no for an answer—this love that you may have rejected, this love that you may have spurned. This love that you said you don't want to be part of your life has come anyway, as sure as the sea rushes the shore. You may think you're too far away; the love of God can never reach you here. Please. You're not even close to the end yet. So while you're breathing and while you're just getting here, take these few moments to relish the love of God that we have in Christ Jesus that simply will not take no for an answer.

Trust Jesus

Your heart and your mind have been so distracted by all of the things that the world throws at you during the day. So let's take a few moments to focus your heart and your mind. I don't know what characteristic of Jesus you want to focus on. There are too many to try to get them all in tonight. You'll have all of eternity to do that. Just grab something. What description? What facet of his personality—Redeemer, Healer, Teacher, Older Brother, Conqueror of death, Peacemaker, Sin Bearer? For me it is the title "Friend." Like a lot of you, I am slow to trust, slow to let someone inside the wall, slow to accept the invitation to be someone's friend. In John 15, Jesus turns to his disciples and says, "I no longer call you servants, but you are my friends" (v. 15, author paraphrase). I can't imagine being with Jesus somewhere as he turns to the person on the other side and says, "This is Mike. He's a friend of mine." But I trust that he does. So you hold your word, and just let it bring you as close to Jesus as you can stand.

Now as close as he is, trust him with the whispers of your heart. All of those superficial things that you pray for, all of those things that come to mind when someone says, "Let's pray," all the formulas, the pocket prayers that we carry—forget that. If we were somehow able to rip the top off of your heart and stick our hand down into your heart as far as we could go, what prayer would we grab? What is the prayer that is so deep and so desired that you dare not even speak it? Will you trust Jesus now and speak it?

Maybe you say it with tears. Maybe with deep sighs. Maybe this ache is so deep, so wide, there are no words. Trust Jesus now to hear what you need to say without you having to say it.

• • •

Dear Father, some of my friends limped in here, wounded and beaten up by life, betrayed by those they trusted deepest, disappointed by dreams that didn't come true, and disappointed most by those dreams that did come true. Some collapsed in their chair; and if they could have found words, their prayer would have simply been, "Help. I can't bear this anymore."

• • •

But you know what it is to be betrayed by friends, to be left alone in the time when you needed someone the most. You know what it feels like to have the whole world get up and walk away—to be branded a loser, a nut, to have everybody shake their head and laugh and leave you. You know what that feels like.

• • •

I don't understand the mystery of how you do what you do. I don't understand the mystery of how you come beside people and help them stand when they don't have the strength. I don't get that. I just know that you're the Shepherd who wouldn't leave one sheep lost, and that after Easter the first person you went looking for was Peter, the one who had failed you hardest.

• • •

Do that now. Cross the miles, cross the time, cross the space, cross the barrier between life and death, and come now to my friends. Call their names. Not the names they were given by the world but the names you gave them before they were formed in the wombs of their mothers, before they gasped their first breath of air. Remind them that though they would consider themselves far off, you would hold them close and dear, maybe rejected by men but chosen by you and precious. A stone rejected by others has become part of the glorious wall glued together by faith, loved by you, the great Cornerstone. Help those who were defeated to stand strong in you in your victory. May those who were lost shout the joy of their homecoming. Oh, that we wounded and broken would rise up on wings of eagles, run and not stumble, walk and not grow weary. Let every step, every moment bring us closer to the time when all the mystery is over and we are lost in you. What we hoped, what we dreamed, what we wished for burns away in the glorious, ultimate, final reality of you. Let life that flows from you flow now to us, and we pray this in the name that is above every name: King of kings, Lord of lords. Amen.

CHAPTER FOUR

The Many Faces of Anger

I was wrapping up a verse-by-verse teaching series on Paul's letter to the Ephesians. On this Tuesday night we were just beginning chapter 6, in which Paul addresses children's relationships to their parents:

> *Children, obey your parents in the Lord, because this is right.*
> *Honor your father and your mother—which is the first command-*
> *ment with a promise—that it may go well with you and that you*
> *may have a long life in the land. And fathers, don't stir up*
> *anger in your children, but bring them up in the training*
> *and instruction of the Lord. (v. 1–4)*

As I began to unpack these verses, making appropriate references to the original Ten Commandments in Exodus, I noticed a darkening of the room. For some reason a dark cloud was beginning to hang over the room. The more I talked, the less they seemed to be willing to listen. I have been speaking for most of my life; like most public speakers I have learned to read an audience. It's a necessary skill to develop if you do what I do. I was reading this audience, and they simply were not buying what I was telling them. They had made up their minds not to keep going with me on the journey because of something I had said, but I didn't know what I had said.

So I interrupted my teaching and asked them why they had stopped listening. There was an uncomfortable shuffling in the room, but no one seemed to be willing to answer my question.

I stepped down from the platform and began to walk through the tables, making direct eye contact with many of them.

"I've been doing this for a long time," I told them. "I know when someone is listening and not listening, and you stopped listening. I want to know why. What did I say that made you pull back?"

No one wanted to answer my question. I kept pressing. There was something going on in the room, and I wanted to know what it was.

"Someone is going to answer my question, or we are going to have a long period of silent prayer."

Finally, one young man mumbled something.

"I'm sorry," I said as I moved over toward him. "I didn't get what you said."

He looked up at me, then looked down again like he really didn't want to repeat what he had said.

"Come on," I pleaded. "You're the brave one. You have the guts to say what everyone else is thinking. Come on, tell me why you quit listening."

"I can't do that," he confessed softly.

"You can't do what?"

"I can't do what you said we have to do."

"Which part?" I asked him. "We've talked about a lot of things."

"That parent thing. I can't honor my parents like that."

"Well, it's not an option," I pointed out. "It's a command. All of us are going to have to find a way to follow this teaching."

He spoke up this time.

"I can't do that, Mike; and if I'm wrong, I'll just have to be wrong."

He looked at me for some kind of assurance that he hadn't stepped over some improper line.

I nodded at him, "Go on."

"My dad left when I was two. For as long as I can remember, it's been just my mom and me. She worked three jobs for most of my life; I worked to put myself through school. I don't even know where my daddy is. I couldn't honor him if I wanted to."

"But Paul is writing . . ."

He didn't let me finish. He pushed his chair back from the table, pointed his finger at me, and shouted, "Listen, Mike, my father never honored me. I'll *never* honor him."

I was stunned. Rarely, if ever, have I seen naked anger expressed that forcefully. His anger was almost primal. While I tried to think about what I would say next, something even more amazing happened.

He got applause.

Across the room people began to clap their hands and nod their heads in support and agreement with this guy's confession. They were all stuck, and they were stuck at the same place. They couldn't, for whatever reason, honor their parents. Because of this gap between what the Bible expected of them and what they were able to do, they felt trapped. They were trapped by their own anger, and they were even angrier because they couldn't get on with their lives.

Surprised by Anger

When people talk to me about Kairos, they usually ask, "What have you learned?" or "What's surprised you?" My answer is always the same: Their anger surprises me. I had no idea these kids carried around that much anger. They are angry with their fathers who left them. They are angry with their mothers for not understanding them. Many of them are angry at the church for not providing the kind of support they needed at some time in their lives. This anger taints every aspect of their lives. It ensnares them into all kinds of self-defeating behaviors and thought patterns.

I don't mean to sound like a pop psychologist, blaming everything on parents. I do believe parents have a profound impact on the lives of their children, and this impact continues well into adulthood. I do believe all of us have to come to some measure of acceptance of who our parents are and, in most cases, come to an appreciation that they tried to love us in the best way they knew how. But what if this acceptance never happens? What if the young adult's relationship is frozen in the last argument they had or, worse, lost in the years of silence after the parent has left?

This anger presents itself in any number of ways. First there is open hostility. Anyone in authority is treated with suspicion and contempt because, "You are not going to do to me what my father did." This anger can be directed at a teacher, supervisor, or even a pastor. Sometimes young adult females will act out their anger in promiscuity, either trying to find the affection and self-esteem they never got from their parents or using sex to punish men for being like their fathers. The anger might present itself as a depression. The young adult, after years of trying but not being able to get what they need from a parent, stops trying at all and withdraws. It might present itself in eating disorders, addictions, and actions to harm themselves. The cavalier "whatever" attitude seen in some young adults is a reflection of anger.

Unfortunately a lot of these young adults have picked up the wrong message from the church and do not feel it is permissible to be angry for any reason at any time. Somehow they picked up the message that good Christians don't get angry for any reason. Anger is to be avoided, pushed out of your life. So no matter what may have provoked the anger, being angry disqualifies you from any moral position in the disagreement. Instead of hearing, "Be angry but do not sin," most heard they were not supposed to be angry, period.

They feel failure on two fronts. First, they don't feel they should be angry at all. Second, they feel they should have the willpower to get past this anger and move on. No one has ever told them that anger is a good, natural, and necessary emotion given by God to his children. They've never learned to deal with the power of the anger. Left uncontrolled, the energy of the anger is channeled in negative and self-destructive ways. Depression, aggression, and failure in relationships—many of the fundamental issues being faced by these young adults can be traced to the corrosive presence of unresolved anger in their lives.

I am not naïve. Our society has developed a convincing game of blaming others for our disappointments in life. Some of these young adults have learned to play the role of victim well. On more than one occasion, we have had to remind young adults that their decisions are their own, that the individual is always responsible for his choices. One of the things that makes Christianity such a difficult way to live is that Jesus never gives us permission to disobey. We can never say to Jesus, "I was hurt, so I wounded my brother," or, "I was tired/angry/down, and that's why I said that to her." Jesus always expects his followers to obey his teachings, regardless of the circumstances.

Rage against the Machine

These are the children of baby boomers; we can't overlook that factor. More than enough research has been printed about the boomers and busters and the difference in their cultures. I will not rehash any of those issues here. Yet the purpose of this book is to point out what we have seen in our experience with Kairos. While we know that lots of boomer parents have done a better than average job, even this seems to have created an underside of pain for the busters—performance anxiety. If both parents are successful, then a certain level of success is assumed for the child. The child is put in the tough position of feeling like no matter what he does, he will never measure up, never be worthy of the parents' love. This quickly turns into a self-loathing; the child will go to extremes of behavior to prove he is unworthy of his parents' love.

The other side of the boomer parent phenomena is that some parents don't want to grow up. They try to be their child's best friend, to relive their youth through the child's activities. Or they simply ignore the fact that they have a child in the first place. The child is seen as a minor and temporary inconvenience who will one day grow up and leave so boomer parents can resume their pursuit of happiness. The child may have been given every material advantage—a car, a good college, great summer trips—but in the end, the child (now a young adult) understands she was viewed as a distraction or interruption to her parents' lives.

Worse, Dad or Mom just left. Most of the young adults at Kairos are the children of divorce. It's one thing to have to deal with challenges of where to spend the holidays or the daily challenges of blended families, but a lot of the young adults I talk to suffer from the anxiety and anger created by having a parent disappear from their lives. There's no question; their parent does not want to be part of their life, does not want the child to be part of the parent's life. The anger from this painful reality ebbs and flows with the tides of the young adult's life. If the young adult is going to school and paying his own way, when the tuition bill is due, he gets angry. If she finds herself facing a complicated life moment, she gets frustrated because no one is around to offer counsel and support.

This rage may be focused on any authority figure in the life of the young adult. A boss, a coach, a professor, or a pastor could be targeted for the transferred anger. As you can imagine, this unfocused and unpredictable rage can work havoc in the lives of young adults today. Some of them have a difficult time keeping a job because they can't get along with their bosses. Add to this the slowing maturation rate in our society, where adolescence is now stretched out to the later twenties or early thirties, and you have a volatile mixture of anger and immaturity.

Not only are young adults frustrated with their parents; they are disappointed in life in general. They are jaded, distrusting any kind of "forever" promises. There's always an expiration date on promises. They have difficulty with long-term relationships, even friendships. Few have long-term career expectations. After all, Mom or Dad may have had a long career with a corporation that said, "Give us your life, and we'll take care of you, no matter what." The parents sacrificed their personal lives on the altar of the corporation, only to be dumped when they were fifty or fifty-five. After years of loyalty on the assembly line, their jobs were shipped to India or Mexico.

This is the first generation of Americans who will not do as well financially as their parents did. And they do not expect to. This makes them angry.

And they are angry at the church. These young adults see the church as being an accomplice of the parent's bad behavior. As one young man told me, "The church we went to knew what my daddy was doing. He ran off, left my mom and me, got remarried, and they elected him deacon. Why didn't they do anything? Why didn't anyone say anything to him? No one cared."

Father's Day

How do we begin to address the issue of anger? The Bible lays out a clear and direct path. As with most things Jesus teaches, it's simple to understand but difficult to do. According to the biblical teaching, if someone has hurt you or you have hurt someone else, you should go to that person and try to restore the relationship. Believe it or not, we have seen this counsel of simple obedience work. Rarely is a broken relationship just the fault of one person. When you start cutting up the blame pie, everyone seems to have a piece. Sometimes the courageous act of calling up someone and offering to talk about the gulf that separates is enough to begin a process of significant healing.

One year, on the Tuesday before Father's Day, we placed Father's Day cards on all of the tables. As we came to the prayer time, I gave them instructions.

"Tonight every one of you is going to write a Father's Day card to your father," I said. "I don't care what's been going on in your life or where you are with your dad. This is the day you're going to begin to deal with all that has happened. If the only thing you can say is, 'I am praying for you,' fine. Write that. Remember, Jesus told us to pray for our enemies. So even if you and your dad are enemies right now, you can still pray for him."

There were more than a few groans across the crowd, but most of them filled out the cards and gave them to us to mail. And we did mail them. Now, not all of these young adults could send their fathers a Father's Day card for obvious reasons. Sometimes the father had died, or in rare situations the father could be dangerous. We did encourage it but left it to their discretion.

One young lady stood around until she was sure she was the last in line at my table afterwards.

"My father started abusing me when I was six," she said. "What do I write?"

The next week several of the young adults came up to me and gave me a report. This had been the first time many of them had been in contact with their fathers for a long time. I think the fathers were as surprised to get the cards as the young adults were to send them. I will never forget one young man who ran up to me before we were getting started with the evening.

"Mike, man, you have to help me."

"What happened?" I asked.

"It's my dad. He called me, man."

"Are you kidding?" I said. "That's great!"

"No, it's not!" he replied. "He wants us to meet. You know, like go out to eat or something. Mike, what am I going to say to him? I haven't seen him in fifteen years, since he packed up and left my mom. What are we going to talk about?"

"Why don't you try asking him how he's doing?" I advised.

There were lots of conversations like that over the next few weeks, and not all of them were happy endings. One young woman showed me a letter in which her father told her he had moved on; he wanted to let the past stay the past, and that included her.

The girl whose father had abused her? She came back to me later.

"I mailed my Father's Day card," she whispered.

"Good for you," I smiled.

"I hope he chokes on it," she replied.

OK, we made some progress. We'll work on attitude for next year. But for the most part things went pretty well with that exercise in obedience. And yes, a few of my young friends brought their fathers to Kairos.

The overall point of Father's Day was that until you can come to some acceptance of your father and mother, you are stuck in many places in your life. We would all wish for parents who would be good models of faith and commitment, and a lot of parents do great work. But when parents don't do this well, the children, now young adults, have no place to go. Feeling alone in the world, they become defensive and suspicious of their surroundings. This makes connecting with faith communities, with God, even more difficult.

I guess that's one of the reasons we have found the practice of the spiritual disciplines so helpful with this age group. Postmodern young adults, as a whole, seek some kind of reconnection with the mystery of life. They have grown suspicious of a faith that can be explained away. So we have found a growing response to liturgical worship and practices. While Kairos would never be mistaken for a liturgical worship service, we do use elements of ancient worship. One of the most effective is the prayer time. Some nights prayer time is the longest element of our time together. We have used ancient prayers of the body (arms raised and open, kneeling, lying down) because doing something with our bodies like kneeling helps us keep our minds and hearts focused. We have also encouraged them to journal as they pray. Something about writing while we pray helps us keep our minds and hearts focused on the moment of prayer. (Many nights I will look out and see them busy at their laptops and

Blackberries. If I didn't know better, I'd think they weren't paying attention. They are. They are journaling as fast as their thumbs can go. They are pondering the verses they've loaded onto their PDAs. They are texting me questions I will have to answer when I get back to my office.)

The challenge for most of us, especially those of us who grew up in Baptist churches, is that we are totally unfamiliar with the classical spiritual disciplines practiced by other Christian traditions. So it may be a good time to start educating yourself on the different types of prayers and how these prayers can be expressed physically as well as mentally and spiritually. Too many of us think that if you move your hands in prayer, you are charismatic. Understand, these are not issues for the people you are trying to reach. Most of them need to have some kind of physical expression to their prayers. Sitting still is not something they do well.

Let me give you an example. I have taught them a practice we call the "prayer of the palms." During this prayer we begin with our hands facing palms down. In this position we are letting things go. We are letting go of anger, self-loathing, bitterness, grudges, wrong thinking, and whatever else keeps us from becoming more like Christ. As you watch them pray, you can actually see people opening and closing their hands as if they are dropping things while they pray. Then, we turn our hands palm upward, ready to receive what Christ would give us in this moment. We open our hands for forgiveness, mercy, healing, hope, and whatever else we may need from Christ in this moment. It is a simple exercise, but remember, we are literally teaching people how to pray. Doing things with their hands is an important teaching tool for them. They are learning how to let go and how to receive.

Putting Away Childish Things

We talk about what it means to forgive. Forgiveness is releasing the other from the expectation that they can fix what they did to you. If I say something to you and hurt your feelings, I may say I'm sorry, I may repent, but it doesn't take the pain out of your heart. Forgiveness comes out of your relationship with Jesus Christ. He's the only one who can heal you. Your dad can't go in there and fix it; your mom can't do it over. But God is not limited by time and space. God is with us in our present. God is already in our future. God is still in our past.

Now here's why this matters: He knows that place in your past that is still bleeding into your present. He can heal it so that it no longer poisons your future. No one had ever told these kids that.

Forgiveness is always a big issue for those who attend Kairos. Sometimes the most intense anger is directed at themselves. Everyone makes mistakes on this treacherous journey from childhood to adulthood. No one gets through adolescence without some scars. The difference is that because our society is forcing our children to grow up so fast, they face much tougher problems at an earlier age. The age most children first encounter drugs has continued to drop, and the first sexual experiences are happening at younger and younger ages. What makes this doubly dangerous is that our children are maturing at a slower rate. My father was a man when he was fourteen. He could work the mules, hitch up the wagon, and drive the neighbor's truck into town for supplies for the farm. I was considered a man when I was twenty-one. Now no one considers you an adult until you have reached the age of thirty. This combination of having to make adult decisions before you are mature enough to think through the consequences has tragic results. Decisions made at fourteen shouldn't affect the rest of your life, but some of those who come to Kairos think they are doing a life sentence for a clumsy decision made in the wilderness of being a teenager in America.

The self-loathing seeps into every area of their lives and poisons whatever it touches. Relationships are wrecked, careers lost, and it all happens because young adults don't believe they deserve the happiness they feel. They are driven to destructive behaviors because they will do almost anything to numb the pain they feel inside.

Most of the objectionable behavior evidenced by the young adults is a symptom of the great pain they feel. Feeling nothing becomes the best alternative.

And sometimes they succeed. They become totally numb. They don't feel anything. They don't feel anything at all.

One night, when we had an open mic, I was walking around the room responding to the questions being asked from the floor. They asked questions all over the board. They wanted to know about forgiveness, not the concept of forgiveness but what it actually is and how you do it in real life. Finally one guy leaning against the back wall spoke up. (We've noticed that there's a progression of attendance at Kairos. The first step is getting there at all. The second step is to go inside, stay at the back of the room, and lean up against the wall so they can take everything in at a safe distance.)

"I don't trust anybody," the voice at the back said. "I'm numb. I don't feel anything at all."

This is where the anger takes them, to a place where they don't feel anything at all. Afraid the anger will explode within them, they turn off the furnace inside and, as a result, turn off everything they feel. They go numb. Nothing makes them happy. Nothing makes them sad. They don't feel. The next step is to do anything to feel something, to feel alive. So girls cut themselves. Guys get into fights. Both young men and young women get inappropriately sexually active, just trying to feel something—anything, even pain—just something to tell them they are still alive.

Leprosy is a disease of the nerves. The body loses its ability to feel pain. Thus, the body is wounded and never knows it. In our overly stimulated desensitizing world, our young adults become numb. Here at Kairos we preach to those who suffer from a leprosy of the heart, to those who have been frozen in their anger. We believe God can raise the dead, and we get together every Tuesday knowing he has plenty of chances.

The Promise:
A Kairos Guided Prayer

Relax

Knowing who you are in Christ, living in the freedom and liberty of who you are uniquely created to be, that's cool. And God defines that. In that court there is no appeal; God said you are cool. He said it by creating you, and he said it by paying the price of his son for you. That makes you universally, eternally cool. Knowing that should make a difference in the way you pray now. Close your eyes; get in a comfortable position. Nobody is moving around but me. Nobody is looking at you but me. This is a safe place. We recognize that you take a certain amount of risk when you come to Kairos. We honor that risk, and we honor that trust. We aren't going to do anything to make you uncomfortable or to put you on the spot in any way. Nobody is sneaking up behind you.

You're just here.

Be Yourself

We invite you here at Kairos to participate in whatever way you are comfortable. In the worship time I have seen some of you lift your hands. If that's who you are, if that's what this moment of worship calls forth in you, by all means do it. I've seen some of you sit quietly and keep your arms folded. That's fine. Wherever you are is where you are. The only thing we ask is that you just keep it real. Be honest. Be honest with yourself. Be honest with God.

Breathe

Breathe all the way in; breathe all the way out. Don't worry about the phone calls you haven't made. Don't worry about things you should have done or what you need to do tomorrow. Just be here in this moment. This is where you are, so just be here. Just breathe.

And as you breathe, remember the promises of God to you. Nothing can separate you from his love. Nothing high above you, nothing deep below you, nothing in the past, nothing in the future, no power, no kingdom, nothing and no one can separate you. There is nowhere you can go where he is not. The psalmist wrote a prayer, "Where can I go where you are not? If I go as high as high is, you are there. If I unroll my sleeping bag in hell you are there" (Ps. 139:7–8, author paraphrase). Remember that in your weakness his strength is made perfect. It is made real. Remember that he did not come to seek those who were already found but to find the lost. The Great Physician did not come for those who were well but to those who were sick and wounded.

Be Grateful

Which promise hit you where you are? What promise did you most need to be reminded of? That he's here? That he's where you are? That there's nothing so big in your life that God can't get over it? That while you may feel like you're the only one in the world, you're not? While you're there, thank him for the promise; thank him for simply being reminded of who he is.

Begin your prayer with praise, applauding God for who he is: Creator, Sustainer, Lover, Forgiver, Redeemer. Don't worry about making it sound pretty. Just pray from your gut.

Let your praise lead you to thanksgiving. You don't have time to thank God for everything. Don't pray like my boys used to pray; they thought by listing everything they could stay up later. Just find one or two things, whatever is significant for you in this moment. Thank God for this.

Be Open

Let your thanksgiving lead you to confidence. I know there is something on your heart and on your mind that you need to talk to Jesus about, and you've been waiting for this moment so you could tell him. Well, tell it. Don't worry about how big it is. Don't edit it to make it acceptable. Just pray it. Trust him to hear what you're trying to say to him. The Bible tells us that the Spirit searches the deep things—goes into your own heart and hears the prayer before it finds words in your mouth, taking that to God, placing it deep in his own heart—so that what you mean is what the Father hears. Trust that. Even if your prayer is nothing but tears, pray it. Trust him.

Now ask the Lord what he needs you to do for him. It may be something simple like calling a sick friend, dropping by a hospital, writing a letter, or baking cookies for a lonely neighbor. It could be a simple thing, or it could be something hard like considering a lifetime of full-time service—maybe internationally, rerouting your life plan a little bit. Some of you may be dealing with some tough stuff right now.

· · ·

God, there are billions of stars, more than we can count. There are more grains of sand on the beach than we ever will be able to number. There are billions of people alive right now, and many are praying right now. There are several hundred praying just in this space alone. But according to the promise in your Word to us, not one word, not one sigh, not one tear, not one laugh has been prayed that you haven't heard. You are answering even before we speak it and answering it in a way that only a Father's love knows best. So we end our prayer now in gratitude. Thank you for being here. Thank you for listening. Amen.

CHAPTER FIVE

Read It, Tell Me What It Means, and Tell Me How I Do It

She was waiting for me as I came into Kairos. As I walked into the foyer of Wilson Hall, a nicely dressed professional young woman approached me.

"Hey, Mike," she said. "I went to LifeWay today."

"Really, what did you get?" I asked.

"Oh, nothing," she replied. "I went looking for a Bible, but I didn't get one."

"Why not?" I asked.

"Mike," she protested, "there are thousands of Bibles in that place. I didn't want to get the wrong one!"

If we have grown up in church, we can forget how confusing just choosing a Bible can be. There are several translations, each one better than the others for particular purposes. Each translation is available in several different styles and formats. There are Bibles with large print, study notes, maps, charts, original leather, and cloth covers. There are Bibles that fold together and snap together in three-ring binders, Bibles with large margins and Bibles with no margins at all, Bibles that are color coded and Bibles with so many notes you can barely find the Scripture in them. Since the Reformation we've had Bibles printed in all kinds of languages. These days we print Bibles to appeal to various demographic subgroups. All of this leads to a mind-numbing confusion that frustrates the first-time buyer of a Bible.

Here we were in Nashville, Tennessee, the buckle of the Bible Belt, and not only did my young friend not have a Bible; she didn't even have the confidence to buy one. Something has happened since Martin Luther determined average men and women could indeed interpret Scripture for themselves. Somehow laypeople in local churches have lost the confidence that they can read and understand the Bible at all. I'm afraid we professional clergy are partly to blame for this. With our insistence on using the "original languages" in our sermons and quoting obscure biblical scholars and theologians to make our points, we have created the illusion that Bible study is for an elite society with a coded language and secret handshake. Most people, if they have a Bible at all, carry it around or read a few favorite passages, but few actually take the time to focus their minds with the intensity required for Bible study. Most people know what the Bible is, but they don't know what the Bible says. They may have been given a Bible by their church when they were children, but they've put it on a shelf somewhere and forgotten about it. They keep it now mainly as a relic of their childhood. The Bible may have some kind of sentimental value to them, but it has no relevant value. They hold onto their Bible because it was given to them by a favorite grandparent or because it reminds them of a simpler time in their own lives, but they do not see any use for the Bible as a guide for living in a postmodern world. When you open up your Bible to begin teaching, you take people into an alien world where few of them have ever ventured. And those that have been there before didn't stay long.

What does that mean for preaching and teaching this post-modern crowd? It means you are going to have to introduce them to the Bible. Then you are going to have to help them get one for themselves. This doesn't mean you have to spend weeks and weeks in the history of the Bible or the theological reasons we consider the Bible to be the revelation of God to us, but you have to introduce them to the Bible the same way you would introduce them to any friend.

How to Buy a Bible

First, and this is not an exaggeration, make sure they have a Bible. Many young adults don't have one. We started leaving copies of the New Testament on the tables at Kairos and around the room. We left paperback copies of the Bible lying around and said, "If you don't have a Bible, take one home with you as our gift."

"Don't worry if you've never read a Bible before," I encourage them. "God has promised to meet us in his Word. His Word does work that we cannot understand until we experience it."

The Bibles have disappeared by the cases. They take one for themselves and come to us holding another one, asking if they can take it to a friend. So what if every one of them isn't being used the way we'd like it to be. We have enough stories of people's lives being changed to more than justify the expense.

The Reformation gave the Bible back to the people. Until Martin Luther and his friends had the audacity to translate the ancient words of Latin, Greek, and Hebrew into the vulgar (or so they were considered at the time) languages of English, German, French, and Spanish, no one but the priests could read the Bible. In fact, people were discouraged from reading the Bible. After all, they didn't have the proper training. In today's church we have created a confusing plethora of translations, styles, and study aids. Every major preacher or teacher has his or her own study Bible. Scholars publish arguments over which translation most accurately reflects the intent of the "original languages." Those of us who make our living in this subculture need to remember that all of this public wrangling over Greek verb tenses and shading of meaning is confusing and unsettling to the people who attend our services and are not as concerned about making it to heaven as they are about making it to next Thursday.

Michael Duduit, the editor of *Preaching Magazine*, is a member of our church. I invited Michael to come and give two presentations on "How to Buy a Bible." The presentation introduced the popular translations, the philosophical foundations that informed the decisions made to complete the translations (cool stuff like dynamic equivalence versus literal translation), and how each translation was intended to be used in biblical study. (By the way, his presentation is on the Kairos Web site. Check it out at www.kairosnashville.com.)

The nearby LifeWay bookstore brought in several tables of displays so that all who were interested could look at each translation and examine every style to find the Bible that best suited them. I will never forget the excitement as, one by one, they would come over to me, show me what they had picked out, and say, "I found my Bible." I have dozens of Bibles in my office, and I can't remember the last time I picked one up, held it to my chest, and said, "This is my Bible!" Like I said, those of us who make our living in the church seem to forget the holiness of these things.

How to Read Your Bible

Now that you are sure they have a copy of the Bible, give them a short reading plan. Help them get started. Most of them have never had someone read the Bible to them, explain a passage, and apply a teaching to their daily lives. When they open the Bible, the first thing that hits them is that they don't get it. To say the Bible is intimidating to the average reader is an understatement. So I begin by walking them through a simple Bible reading plan.

Start with the Gospel of Mark. Mark was most likely written first; it's the shortest of the Gospels. Mark's goal was to tell the story of Jesus as fast as he could. Mark's favorite word seems to be "immediately." Mark has few transitions and even less in the way of explanation. "Here is what Jesus said and did," Mark seems to say. "Now believe."

Read the Bible slowly, I tell them. You are going to be reading the Bible the rest of your life, so you probably have sixty or seventy more years to get through the rest of it. When you read a passage and it makes you think, stop and write about it in your journal. I have found keeping a journal to be one of the most rewarding spiritual disciplines in my own life, and I strongly encourage my young friends to develop this holy habit. Something about holding a pen in your hand forces your mind to stay focused on the matter in front of you. Writing out your prayers is a great way to keep your mind from wandering. This is an important skill for new readers of Scripture to learn.

Once they get through Mark, I tell them to reread Mark. According to people who stay up late at night and study these things, people don't retain most of what they read for the first time. Rereading is important if the content of the Bible is to be ingrained into their lives. After they have read and reread Mark, I tell them to read Matthew and Luke. Again, read slowly, and read them more than once. Then read the Gospel of John. John is the poet of the Gospel writers; he never lets details get in the way of making the point that Jesus is the Word become flesh. Next I tell them to read Acts. After Acts, read the letters of Paul and then the other epistles to the church in the New Testament. I tell them to put off the book of Revelation until they are old and retired. John wrote the book when he was an old man, and it needs to be read by people with a lot of life experience to help them understand it. Revelation is one of my favorite books, but it needs to be read and interpreted with great patience and discernment, or the reader ends up finding the number 666 everywhere and the Antichrist behind every tree.

The point is to get them started. I don't care what version of the Bible they use. I don't care if it has maps or not. I just want to get them to read the Bible, any Bible, any way I can. There is no such thing as a bad Bible. Just start.

To make my point, I ask them to make me a promise: read one word a day. That's it. Just one word. I know what will happen. They will become curious and read a whole paragraph, maybe even an entire chapter. But if I tell them that, it will frighten them. So I say, "Read one word." They don't believe that will work, so I ask them to tell me what the first word of the Bible is.

"In!" someone shouts.

That's right, "In the beginning." Now, if we have an *in*, we have to have an *out*. Who's in? Who's out? Isn't that what the whole Bible is about? Of course, this is simple. I know there's more to Bible study than this. I know you can spend the rest of your life plumbing the depths of Scripture. This is one of the wonders of the Bible. The child can read it and understand it while scholars can be intrigued for their entire careers by just a few passages.

The main thing is to get them started anywhere with any Bible. The Bible is totally new to them and to the pattern of their living. They are used to texting, e-mailing, surfing the Web, and watching YouTube videos. Reading the Bible is not something they think about naturally or are encouraged to do by the culture. But I am confident in the Bible's ability to hold the attention of believers' minds and hearts once they are introduced. They can read the Bible online and on their PDAs. They can listen to it on their iPods. Find a way to get it into their hearts.

I know you're thinking, *Hey, I thought this guy was writing a book about how to reach postmoderns. All he's talking about is simple expository preaching and teaching.*

You're right. That's what I am talking about. And you're right again; that doesn't seem to be too radical. I can't say it too many times: most of these young people have never read the Bible at all. Everything in it is new to them. They don't know this is where we get the Ten Commandments. They don't know Abraham or Isaac, Jacob or Daniel. They may have heard the story of David and Goliath, but, like Jack and the beanstalk, they thought these were fables told to them so they wouldn't give up when they faced overwhelming odds. They had no idea David was a real person, a real king.

What It Means and How To Do It

This brings me to an important point: you can't assume anything in your teaching. When you reference a Scripture passage, you have to quote it or read it. They will not be familiar with it. You'd think that growing up in the Bible Belt, these young people would be conversant with at least the basic stories of the Bible. They are not. This startling reality hit me between the eyes in a meeting we were having with a focus group.

Things were not going well. In the beginning, despite our best energies, Kairos was having a hard time gaining any traction. I couldn't understand why. There are books and more books about how to do church in a way that attracts postmoderns. We were doing all of the cool stuff the experts said we should do. The lighting was cool. The staging was cool. What was missing? As I talked to them about what we were trying to do, they began to shake their heads. Finally one young man spoke for the group.

"Mike, we don't want any of that," he said.

"Well, what do you want?" I asked.

"I want you to read it, tell me what it means, and tell me how to do it."

"But that's not creative," I protested.

"Read it, tell me what it means, and tell me how to do it," he insisted. "We've never heard this before."

Never heard this before? Was he kidding? Were they kidding? No, they weren't kidding at all. Many of these young adults had grown up in church. Some of them had grown up in *my* church. And now here was the heartbreaking truth: they didn't know the Bible. They had attended youth groups that majored on entertainment or "rap sessions" where we sat around in circles and talked about things that were going on in our lives. For some reason we thought teenagers listening to the opinions of other teenagers was the way to grow disciples. Certainly you couldn't get students to come and study the Bible. At least no one thought so. The result? An entire generation, maybe two, who are not grounded in their faith and have no idea why they believe what they believe, who have no framework of thought to engage the world. If the Bible is the sword of our armor that Paul described in Ephesians 6, then our young people have been sent out into the battle unarmed.

At Kairos we preach and teach the Bible from cover to cover. We have gone through Mark and Ephesians; we have studied the stories of Joseph, David, and Daniel; walked through Exodus; and now we are in the Gospel of John. Their response? Well, it's been interesting. They loved Joseph. Who knew there were dysfunctional families in the Bible?

"His brothers sold him? Are you kidding? I beat up my brother once or twice, but I never sold him."

And they learned about forgiveness. What would you have done if you were Joseph and found your brothers bowing before you begging for food?

We learned that no one is perfect.

"David had an affair? Really? And then what happened?"

Funny, these postmoderns think immorality is a recent invention.

Nicodemus and the woman at the well, Peter and the rest of the disciples, Adam and Eve, Moses and Joshua, Rebekah and Ruth—all of their stories are told so that we can see how human they were. People just like us got in and out of messes, made mistakes and tried to fix them, and through it all God was working his will toward the promised redemption of creation.

And you know what? If God can work through Peter and the rest of them, maybe he can work in me.

"Did he forgive David?"

Yes, he forgave David. In fact, David's prayer is in the Bible.

"It is? Where?"

"Psalm 51:10, 'Create in me a clean heart, O God'."

"That was his prayer? Really? Can I pray this prayer?"

"Yes, you can." And they do, and God does. And next week I'll tell them to open their Bibles, and we'll pick up where we left off.

Sometimes we who make our living as religious professionals forget to trust the power of the Word. We think we have to jazz it up, or it just won't work with sophisticated and jaded media-savvy postmoderns. We're wrong. They can know truth when they hear it. They're hungry for it. They see the validity of Scripture, how the Bible describes life and points out the things that matter today, that have always mattered. These same things will matter tomorrow. And this determined commitment to the truth resonates with Kairos. The Bible tells them the truth about people, about themselves, and about life. The names may be a little funny and the customs sometimes hard to understand, but the reality is, despite all of our technological advancements, people haven't really changed all that much. These young readers recognize themselves in the faces of the Bible characters. Their story is our story.

Recently, teaching in Daniel, I talked about Nebuchadnezzar losing his mind.

"You don't think this happened in the Bible," I said, "but I can tell you story after story of people who did the same things you do to get their next drug, their next fix, their next good feeling. This is what happened to Nebuchadnezzar."

I came up with a phrase to describe this: Monkey Mind.

"Part of your brain deals with your urges and your desires," I said as I drew a picture of a brain on the board. "That's your Monkey Mind; it's your inner animal. When you see something you want and have to have it, when you can be 'in love' tonight and 'out of love' in the morning, you are thinking with your Monkey Mind."

I used Monkey Mind to describe what was happening to Nebuchadnezzar, and we got twenty-five to thirty e-mails the next morning saying, "Monkey Mind is where I'm at."

"I'm going to stop right here in Daniel," I said the next Tuesday. "We're going to deal with this Monkey Mind thing because you think it's a new idea. It's not."

We read Paul's teaching in Romans about the old nature and the new nature. We read Romans 7, in which Paul laments that he is at war with his members.

"Do you get what he is saying?" I asked. "You've been in church too long. He's saying, 'I've got body parts that don't listen to Jesus.' That's Monkey Mind, an old concept you knew intimately. You just didn't know what to call it."

By encouraging these young adults to engage the Bible at this level, we help them to begin to construct a biblical worldview. This process takes longer for some of them because they have to spend some serious time deconstructing the worldview they have unconsciously built as they engaged the culture around them. They have a worldview; everyone does. They don't know they have a worldview, and they don't know what their worldview is or how it affects them as they make decisions. Things they have learned from their parents, the entertainment industry, and college professors they simply took as truth. (Remember, there was no counter claim of truth in most of their lives.) They've never critically examined what they believe or why they believe it. What works with nonbelievers also works with disenfranchised believers. We made the assumption that they have heard this stuff, and they haven't. That's what the unbeliever and the reclaimed church member have in common: they don't know anything.

When the Bible begins to reveal the truth of the living God to these young readers, their whole lives begin to change. You see it first in the way they think about themselves. They no longer judge themselves by the capricious standards of society. They begin to see the value in loving ourselves as commanded by Christ and the treasure of the *imago Dei* that each of us bear.

They begin to treat one another differently. They see their jobs differently, and many of them become better employees because they are bringing better attitudes into the workplace. All of this happens when they begin to read the Bible.

The Word of God is living and active. Trust it. Remember that the important thing is to get them started reading it—anywhere, anytime, in any version. Starting is always the hardest part. So just start.

The God Who Is:
A Kairos Guided Prayer

Welcome

If this is your first time at Kairos, let me be one of the first to welcome you. We invite you to participate in the worship and in the study at whatever level you feel good. Whatever is real for you is what we want for you. What I don't want is your looking around trying to figure out how everybody else is doing it and trying to do it that way—kind of like when you eat at a fancy restaurant and you don't know which fork to use, so you watch and see what everybody else is doing, assuming it is right.

When we talk about the Kairos service, you tell us over and over again that one of the most important things that happens is this prayer time. For some of you, it's the only time during the week that you are still and quiet. I hope that you are learning that you can do this by yourself. You don't have to come on Tuesday night and hear me lead you through it. I hope I'm teaching you some things that you can do by yourself. If you check the Kairos Nashville Web site, you'll see we've added the prayer times as separate pod casts, so it's something you can do at home alone. Just download them and get used to doing this on your own.

Draw Close

Get in a comfortable position, take a deep breath, and close your eyes. The only reason I want you to close your eyes is that I don't want you distracted by anything going on around you. I don't know about you, but right now, particularly on this day, this Tuesday, I just don't feel God a whole lot. You may think I just walk around in constant one-on-one conversation with God. I don't. But my relationship with God, my proximity to him, is not determined by my emotions at the moment, not by how I feel. Emotions are important, but we do not make our decisions by them. The relationship that we have—that I have, that you have with God—is based on his promise to you. It's the promise he gave to you in the person of Jesus Christ, who died for you and was raised from the dead, and who now in the person of his Spirit lives among you, even in you. That's his promise to you, and it doesn't change with the weather, with the rise and flow of culture or circumstance. God's Word depends on one thing and only one thing: God.

Believe

With this in mind, I want to help you remember some things God promised you in his Word, things you can count on. The first one is one of the first of the Ten Commandments.

God told Moses to write down, "You shall have no other gods before me." Now we always read that as a bad thing, as a rule we have to keep. But maybe God was telling Moses, "Listen, I'm the only God there is. Don't put anything else in the place where only I can be."

His first promise to you is that *he is*. Before the universe, before time, when the sun burns out, when the planets no longer rotate in their orbits, when the last star has fizzled, God still is.

Now while you're trying to get your mind around that incredible fact, push it just a little further and hear the promise that *nothing* can separate you from the love of God that we have in Christ Jesus—not anything on the earth, not anything above, not anything below, not anything in the past, not anything in the future. Not any government, not any spiritual powers—not one thing can separate you from the God who is. Maybe you're like me, and you're not feeling too in touch with God. That's OK. The promise still stands. Nothing separates you.

Pluto is so far away from the sun that the sun's rays never really warm it. It is frozen all the time. We measure the distance from the sun to Pluto in light-years. Even if you were to catch the next shuttle to Pluto, at no point along your journey, even after landing on Pluto, would you ever be out of his presence. That's a promise.

Confess

In 1 John the writer tells us, "If we are faithful to confess our sins, he is faithful to forgive them" (1:9). Confession is not a time to beat yourself up. That's not what it's about. It's the time to get real and honest with yourself and with Jesus. You can't deal with it until you name it. This is the time to name it: "This is who I am; this is what I've done; this is what's going on. This is the beast I'm dealing with." Nothing can separate you from God, not even your own mistakes. So in the confidence of God's Word to you, confess your sins to him.

Ask

Jesus promised, "Ask and you will receive. Knock and it will be opened to you. Seek and you will find" (Matt. 7:7, author paraphrase). James reminds us, "You have not because you ask not." So ask. Ask for your friends, for people you love. We call that intercession.

Ask for Kairos and the leaders of Kairos. Ask for this church, if this is where you go; or ask for the church where you attend. Pray for the leaders of your church.

Pray for yourself, not so much this list of needs or wants that you have, but ask what Jesus wants of you. Many times our prayers are not dialogues, they're monologues. We are telling Jesus everything that is going on. Rarely do we take the time to listen to what he would ask of us.

Celebrate the Moments

As we conclude our time here, I want you to think back. Think back to those significant markers in your life, those significant times. Sometimes you only see God in hindsight. Think about the moment when you thought you were all by yourself and God sent someone to find you. Or you happened to run into somebody, or you happened to pick up a book. Or the Scripture happened to fall open to a particular story. And now as you look back, even after all of these years, you see that God was there all the time.

For all of those moments, give thanks. Let your thanksgiving lead you to confidence and boldness, knowing that nothing that happens tomorrow will pull you away from him. Nothing that happens next year or at any point of your life will pull you away from him. And this same Jesus who has been with you all the time is with you now, here in this moment. He's healing, forgiving, loving, encouraging, celebrating, and laughing because nothing can take you away from him.

● ● ●

*Father, as we welcome you now into this service, welcome us into
your presence. Awaken us so that we will know that
you are closer than the air we breathe; and if you are indeed
here, then everything is all right. Regardless of how we feel,
regardless of what we are going through, it's all right.
Let us relax in the joy and confidence of knowing that
you are a Savior who keeps his promises. Amen.*

CHAPTER SIX

Groups: The Family Reconstituted

Connie Lunceford is well into her eighties. She and her husband, Art, have been married for sixty-seven years. I got to know Art and Connie at a luncheon celebrating couples in our church that had been married for fifty years. Art had shown me a picture of him and Connie, stiffly posed on their wedding day.

"Do we look a little rushed, Preacher" he had asked me.

"Well, Art," I said, "you do look a little nervous."

"Her grandfather was chasing us with a shotgun. He found out Connie and I were going to get married, and he was coming after us."

I still laugh when I think about that story. Connie and Art are great people, solid in their convictions and living life to the fullest. So I don't guess I should have been surprised when I walked into Kairos and saw Connie and a few of her friends sitting in their chairs waiting for the service to begin.

"Connie," I said, "what are you doing here?"

"I've just heard about Kairos and everything happening here, so I thought I would come and see for myself."

As we started the evening, I introduced Connie to the young adults who were there that night. When I told them that Connie and Art had been married for sixty-seven years, they started to applaud. The applause grew louder and louder and, to my surprise, they gave Connie a standing ovation. After Kairos was over, young adults, especially the young women, flocked around Connie as if she were a rock star. I saw Connie the next Sunday, and she just couldn't get over all of those young people and how much love she had felt from them. I tried to explain to Connie about how important her presence had been to Kairos.

"You are living proof," I said. "They hear all of the time about commitment and what Jesus can do in your life, but they rarely get to see it."

Kairos had looked at Connie and said, "Ah, this is what it looks like to walk after Jesus for a long time. This is what it looks like to stay married all of your life. It can happen. Maybe it can happen to me just like it did for her."

The Failure of Family

Most of us have read the statistics about the disintegrating family. Many studies put the national divorce rate at 50 percent or higher. Some parents get married more than twice and their children, no matter what age they may be, have to adjust to—sometimes endure—their blended families. There are lifelong implications. Commitments are seen as something that can be ignored or jettisoned when the requirements of the promises become personally inconvenient. Those children of divorce, now young adults, are trying to find their own relationships but doubt whether they can find anything that will really last. This is one reason talking about abstinence is so difficult. When you talk to young people about waiting to engage in sexual intercourse, they don't think there is anything to wait for. Most young adults at Kairos don't believe the idea that there is a person who will love them for the rest of their lives. They've never seen anyone love in a committed fashion, not their parents and not the parents of their friends.

Critical life skills are not being passed down. For many generations sons would work with their fathers on the family farm. During these long hours of taking care of the chores, a lot of conversations would take place. A lot of life truths would be passed down from father to son. The rhythm of farm life provided ample opportunities for life lessons as they were needed. Likewise, daughters helped their mothers with the family chores, and there were plenty of opportunities for conversations. I know I'm oversimplifying, perhaps even romanticizing life on the farm. I know life wasn't that easy. The point I'm trying to make is this: families used to do more things together—working together, socializing and attending church together—and these opportunities were where children learned from their parents and other significant adults what it meant to be grown up. The group of influential adults would include parents, grandparents, uncles, aunts, other extended family, and friends of the family. Some of these family friends would have known the parents since childhood. A consistent message of connectedness and community was reinforced on multiple levels.

Now dads travel and moms go to work. The kids are busy in school and after school. By the time everyone gets home, there's just time to throw something in the microwave and veg out in front of the television for an hour or so. That is, of course, if the children aren't in their own rooms on the Internet or playing digital games. Unless the parents are intentional and disciplined about the process, meaningful conversations with their children simply will not happen.

If these conversations did happen, what good would they do? The world is changing so fast, in some ways parents can't help their kids, or so we are told. But I've found that as much as the world continues to change, a lot of it seems to stay the same. Despite all of the changes in the digital world, people are still much the same. Children need their parents to be proud of them. They need the unconditional love of a mother and father, and they still need someone to trust as they go through the world. With so many parents physically and emotionally absent, the child is left unprotected on several levels.

Several years ago John Trent and Gary Smalley wrote a classic book entitled *The Blessing*. According to this book children look for their parents to pass the blessing to them. This blessing consists of several parts: the unconditional love for the child, the parent's commitment to the child's future, the spoken word of encouragement, and touch. This blessing is part of the child's heritage, and as their future unfolds, the power of the blessing propels them toward it.[4]

One Tuesday night after our prayer time, a young man stepped up to my table.

"Will you pray for me, Mike?" he asked.

"Anything in particular, or just everything in general?" I replied.

"I'm getting married in two weeks."

"Great!" I smiled.

"I hope so," he said.

"Hope so? You're a little late for 'hope so.'"

"I love her," he replied, "and she keeps telling me how excited she is that we're getting married. She can't wait for me to be the spiritual head of our house. Mike, I don't know what the spiritual head of the house is! I'm scared to death!"

"I'm going to pray for you," I told him. "Then I'm going to introduce you to some folks who've been married for about forty years, and they are going to mentor you."

Senior Link

They show up at Kairos with lots of baggage, and we discovered we had nowhere to unload it. The pastoral care load would be impossible for an entire team of trained counselors, much less the staff of a local church. We needed to recreate the family structure. We needed to put sons with fathers and daughters with parents. Grandparents needed to find new grandchildren. This, of course, is not anything new to the church. In the first century (even now in parts of the world) when you became a Christian, your family disowned you. What was a person to do? To be without family or home meant losing your work and social safety net. Some young men and women suddenly became homeless. So the early church would assign new believers to new families. Christian fathers and mothers would "adopt" the younger believers in the Christian community and raise them as their own children. These new believers were taught how to live in a pagan world as Christians. Older men taught younger men; older women taught younger women. The faith and the required skills for life were passed down from generation to generation.

To create this family structure for Kairos, Cathy Patterson began meeting with the senior adult ministry of Brentwood Baptist Church. With their support and insight, she designed a ministry called Senior Link.

At Senior Link, we take senior adults and pair them up with singles and young couples from Kairos. We do a survey on life experience, hobbies, professional experience, even favorite sports teams and other points of connection. A team matches them up. Then we invite them to a dinner at the church to make our Senior Link connections. We introduce the senior adult and the young adult and seat them at a table with a list of questions to get the conversation started. Most of the time the questions aren't needed. The young adults are delighted to have someone truly interested in their lives, and the senior adults are impressed to have someone who will listen to their life stories and learn from them.

After the dinner what happens is up to them. Some follow up with phone calls and an occasional dinner. Others end up fulfilling the duties of family members, including helping the senior adult get to the doctor. One young person from Kairos insisted the

Senior Link be introduced to the new fiancé when the couple got engaged.

Guy and Garnett are senior adults in Brentwood Baptist Church. Cindy was their Kairos adoptee. When Guy and Garnett first got together with Cindy, she was not a believer. Guy and Garnett welcomed her into their home and their lives, and in the course of their time together, Cindy began to ask questions. Guy and Garnett began to send me e-mails to pray as they talked about Christ and his gospel.

One Sunday after the service, as I waited in a parlor where we receive new members and counsel those who are making decisions, Guy came in and started looking around anxiously.

"Is she here yet?" he asked.

"I don't know, Guy. Who are you looking for?"

"Cindy! She's going to make her profession of faith today. You can't leave until she gets here."

"I'll wait," I promised.

In a few minutes Garnett came in with Cindy. As Cindy told me the story of how she had come to faith in Jesus Christ, I couldn't help but notice Guy and Garnett standing directly behind Cindy. They were there to support her, to be part of this important morning; and they looked just like parents do when they bring their children back to meet me after a service. Both Guy and Garnett were wiping away tears. For all anyone knew who might have been watching the scene, this was a couple standing there with their own daughter. She was their daughter. In Christ she had been given a new family.

Not every family is traditional. Sue is retired from denominational life. Shana is a young hot shot in the advertising industry. Sue never married and has no children of her own, but she has worked in preschool and children's ministries all of her life, so you could say she literally has thousands of children she would call her own. Shana was new in Nashville; finding a friend like Sue was important for her. Because Sue is single and retired, she can travel on a moment's notice, so she and Shana have become great travel buddies. When our church sent a mission team to Thailand, the two of them went early and planned a side trip to a nearby village to meet the child they had adopted together through a world hunger relief agency. Sue loves to cook, and she is teaching Shana. Shana loves animals; now Sue has a dog. Over and over we see the blessing come true: "Once you were not a people, but now you are the people of God" (1 Pet. 2:10 NIV). In Christ people are given the families they need for the journey of life and for their growth as disciples.

It doesn't always work out like this. Sometimes the young people will just fade away, change their e-mail addresses and cell phone numbers, change jobs and apartments. One of the great things about being single is that you can pick up and move in a moment's notice. The bad thing about dealing with singles is that they can pick up and move faster than you can update a databank. If a company comes out with a special cell phone package, they'll change every number they have and never let us know. That's just the nature of this demographic.

Group Homes

Small groups are also part of this family-creating process. Small groups are groups of three to eight people who meet together for Bible study, mutual encouragement, and accountability. This is especially important for young men. Young men run in packs anyway, and it's important that we give young men packs of positive influences. Few young men can be faithful to the Christian walk without support, but they can be strong when they learn they have other young men counting on them. We train leaders of small groups three or four times a year and open up the small groups several times a year. When we do, we spend a lot of time talking about the purpose of the groups. The groups exist to help us grow as disciples and to find a few good friends who will become brothers and sisters. As much as possible we try to keep the groups divided, men only or women only. We've found that conversation will be much deeper without the added pressure of someone from the opposite sex being part of the conversation. We also insist that the groups focus on the study of Scripture. I know there are a lot of good books out there. I have a library full of them. But for reasons we have talked about in other parts of this book, we've found most of the young people we deal with to be biblically illiterate. We need to get them engaged in meaningful Bible study in whatever way we can.

Most of our groups meet in either the church or local restaurants. As you can imagine, not many of the young adults have a place large enough to host a small group. We've also seen that people are hesitant about meeting in someone else's home until some kind of relationship is established. We do have some older couples that host groups in their homes and teach the group together. While not part of Senior Link, this type of small group serves some of the same purposes. A family group is established, and life skills as well as Christian truths get passed down.

We have found it important to have at least one open group. An open group is designed for people to drop in and out. Each night's lesson stands on its own and is not connected to the one before or the one after. Brian and Rachel host a group called "forty-one." According to Brian, he came up with the name "forty-one" when he realized that everything in the Bible lasted forty days or forty years. Because of this, Brian thinks the number forty-one stands for moving on, starting over. After forty days in the wilderness, on day forty-one, Jesus started his ministry. Brian is a computer consultant, and Rachel is a musician. They are the parents of two boys, so their home is a place of high energy and genuine hospitality. Brian has the ability to get to the heart of a matter in a short period of time. People enjoy being able to come to this small community and determine their level of involvement in the safe way an open group provides.

Getting young adults involved in small groups at a significant level is a difficult process. In many ways the small group process has been the slowest part of Kairos to develop. Young adults are slow to trust and even slower to open up and reveal what is going on in their own lives. Working to gain this trust takes a long time. There is no way to speed it up or make it go faster. I guess this is why Jesus talked so much about agriculture. You plant the seed, you water it, and you wait. Sometimes the crop comes in, and sometimes it doesn't; but when the crop does come in, the harvest is something else. Small groups are an absolute necessity for growing authentic disciples of Christ.

Special Needs

As you develop small groups in your ministry, you may find out you need special groups to take care of critical situations that will be part of the ministry. We have found it important to have at least three special emphasis groups led by mature, experienced, and well-trained leaders who can respond effectively to someone who is hurting. Dealing with divorce, abuse, or coming out of addiction requires a special insight and compassion level by the leader. You need to be proactive about having these groups set up and ready. When the person comes to you for help, make the connection quickly. Waiting can prove to be disastrous and rapidly decreases the chances of a successful recovery. With prayer you will find people of extraordinary mercy and grace who will be able and ready to handle the spiritual and emotional refugees of our world.

This reconnection to family structures is especially important for young adult men. While studies are now confirming that young adult women are expressing their own struggles in a variety of ways, young men have been uniquely damaged by the disintegration of the American family. In particular, the absence of fathers means that in critical moments in their lives, the moments when they needed someone to mentor them in the ways a man handles his life, these guys had no one there. Some turn to gangs, and the results are well documented. Some look to the media for heroes with, let's say, mixed results. Most just end up lost.

We are now dealing with our second generation of young men who have had no significant positive male role models impacting their lives. This is why we get excited when men volunteer to work in the preschool and children's ministries of our church. For many children the man they see in the nursery on Sunday may be the only man they relate to all week. With no male role models, a young man has no idea how to relate to God as Father. With no male role models, a young man has no idea how to relate to women in either dating relationships or marriage. They have no idea what it means to be a father. The reason we have so many deadbeat dads is that many of these men do not know what a father is supposed to do. The responsibility of molding the life of a child is just too much for many young men to fathom. Many young men were raised by a single mother or raised by a grandmother while their mother worked. (Why does every professional athlete who gets his face on the television wave and say, "Hi, Mom?" Why does no one say hi to dad? Dad wasn't there.) We need to commend the number of single mothers who, through enormous personal sacrifice, support and raise successful, healthy young men—women who make tremendous contributions to our churches and society. Yet we also have to admit we have at least one generation of young men who are desperate to find out who they are and for what purpose they were created. Churches need to be restructured to give strong men of faith ample time to spend with young men. They don't need to spend a lot of time in committees. They need to invest in mentoring relationships. This, too, is effective Christlike leadership.

This may be one of the most important ministries of the church: reconstituting the family for the orphans of our culture. As we are discovering, you can be an orphan even if both parents are living. As mature Christians invest time and godly wisdom in the lives of young adults, anger is dissipated, wounds are healed, grudges are forgiven and released, crucial life skills are learned, and young adults find their identity in their relationship to Jesus Christ. If we can do this, we will begin to reverse the trend of children who wander the world without a parent to guide them to their true selves.

Today the postmodern church is going to have to rediscover the ancient practice of spiritual adoption. It is a rescue mission. Young people will never understand God's love for them until they see the love of God embodied in the life of a mature believer who is willing to give them the most important gift of all, their attention.

Polarities:
A Kairos Guided Prayer

Come In

When I was in seminary, one of my professors had written a book called *Polarities of Man's Existence in New Testament Perspective*. So most of us bought the book, put it on our shelf, looked at it, and said, "What?" What we learned when we started reading the book was that Christians live between two poles most of the time: saint and sinner, alive yet dying, dead but living again—all of these polarities. And we bounce back and forth between this good news/bad news, tough times/good times most of the days of our lives. Tonight is a good example. As we came in the door, we had people directing a group of people to the sanctuary where visitation was being held for a member of our church who passed away. In this room we are celebrating life with all of its potential and promise, and on the other side of the building we are celebrating a life that is finished. Polarities.

Today a friend e-mailed me a picture of his brand-new baby boy. I looked for razor burns on this boy. He must be shaving. This baby was huge. Huge! Just a few minutes before I came down here, I got a call from another friend who is dealing with addiction and is having a hard time staying on the wagon. The Bible says you celebrate with those who celebrate, you rejoice with those who rejoice, and you grieve with those who grieve. You're always in these polarities. I guess that's why we love Psalm 139 so much, that passage where David asks,

"Where can I go from your spirit? If I make my bed in hell you are there, if I ascend to the highest heights you are there" (v. 7–8, author paraphrase). We live somewhere between those places most of the time, don't we?

You Are Here

Wherever you are on that continuum, whatever polarity you are drawn to or bouncing in between, it's OK. Where you are is where you are. And I'm going to give you permission where you are to close your eyes, get in a comfortable position, take a deep breath, and get a feel for where you are. Check your spiritual GPS real fast: "This is where I am, this is what I'm going through, this is what I'm facing, this is what I'm dealing with. This is what is right, and I want to celebrate; this is what I'm struggling with, and I want to pray through it." Do this fast. Don't hold onto any detail too long. Just get a fast reading of where you are. Just where you are. You are here.

Can you put it in different buckets? Can you sort it really fast? This is a good thing, this is a praise, that's a prayer concern, and this is something I'm struggling with. Can you throw it into buckets real fast? Go ahead and do it. Don't analyze it; just do it.

What's Good?

I want you to grab that bucket of good things. Don't tell me you don't have anything in your bucket. I'm just not going to buy that. Maybe you need to think a little harder, look a little deeper, and find out what is in your life that you can put in your bucket. Grab one or two of them, and say, "You know, this is really a good thing."

I'm grateful that I have friends who make me laugh. They'll call me to see how I'm doing and really mean it, and then they'll tell me something funny they've just seen or just heard. Sometimes in the middle of my day the best thing I can do is just laugh. I'm grateful for that.

Are there any surprises in the bucket? Are there things that used to be not so good, but now you can say, "Hey, this is a good thing"? It's kind of like eating your spinach; it's something, a gift from God that you didn't recognize at first as being good, but now you see it is. Take a few moments. Give thanks. Celebrate because we are going to use this in just a minute.

What's Hard?

Now look at that bucket of hard things, the bucket that causes you pain and grief. I'm not mentioning this to you so that you can focus on it. Some of us will lock in on the bad stuff. It's all we'll think about. Of ten things in our life, if nine things are going right, we will fixate on the one thing going wrong.

Life always is that mixture. But I know some of you hurt. Some of you are in job transitions. Some of you are lonely; some of you have just broken up. Some of you have gotten the job you always wanted. Now you're scared you're not going to be able to do it. You just had a baby; you just got married. You have started one of these life transitions, and all of a sudden life has gotten serious. Now there's a grief in that, and that's OK. The God that provided all those good things in your life is the same God that is listening to you now about what's hurting. If he was powerful enough to do a good thing, he will be powerful enough to handle the problems too. Remember, if you make your bed in hell, he's already there.

What's Ahead?

You should have another bucket, a bucket of something you desire, hope for, dream about. Maybe this dream is so deep that you don't even tell anybody about it. Bring that out. Pray about it. Offer your dream to the Lord as an offering, as a sacrifice. Offer it to him to use in his kingdom in whatever way he chooses so that it is no longer your dream now but his.

I told you about the hand prayer before, didn't I? Remember when your hands are out in front of you and turned palms down, you are letting go of things. When they are turned palms up, you are receiving. Let go of anger, let go of grief, let go of your mistakes and failures. Receive forgiveness, receive healing, receive hope.

Here's the last part of that prayer. Just rest your hands in your lap. Comfortable? Just relax. Trust the Father to take care of you now. Surrender to his will. Remember, the hardest part of swimming is learning how to float. This is the time I am teaching you how to float. Inhale, exhale, and relax. Float in the love that will not let you go.

● ● ●

Lord, some of my friends are in the best times of their lives, so hear their praise and celebration. Clap and sing with them. Some are in their worst moment ever. Hear their tears. Weep with them. All of us—those who rejoice and those who despair— all of us ask the same thing: come be with us. We don't mind the mountain. We don't mind the battle. What we need most of all is for you simply to be where we are. That will be answer enough. And we pray this in your name. Amen.

CHAPTER SEVEN

The Risk of Honest Struggle

When you pastor a local Baptist church, some weeks are harder than others. This had been a hard week. Earlier that morning I had presided over the funeral of an infant. He suffered from a serious birth defect that made it impossible for him to live more than a few hours after he was born. Even sadder, this condition had been discovered while he was still in his mother's womb, but she had decided to carry him to full term. We had been walking down this road for several months, and when he was born, we held him for a few moments until he died. Already mentally, physically, and spiritually exhausted from the previous months, now we had to plan a funeral and walk with this family while we laid their child to rest. Funerals of children are the hardest part of my job. Nothing else comes close. After a situation like this, I'm exhausted, and this day was no different. I was almost numb by the time I left the family's house in the early afternoon. Now I had to lead Kairos.

I didn't feel like leading Kairos. The last thing I wanted to do was to stand up and smile and say, "God loves you." I was angry about what my friends had endured. I wanted God to answer some questions. I wanted God to come down, sit in front of me, and give an accounting for why he let things get this screwed up. As in other moments like this in my life, God didn't answer at all, and maybe that's a good thing. Maybe his silence at these times is the silence of a good friend who just ignores you when you say something stupid.

My mind was fried from the events of the day, and I was having difficulty concentrating. How was I going to preach? I had a message prepared, but I couldn't think clearly enough to remember it.

I took a risk. I put a stool in the middle of the stage, and I sat on it. I looked out at them and told them about the day, everything that had happened. I told them about my anger at God, my fatigue, and my frustration because I did not have the answers when life had hard questions. I confessed that I have some days when, frankly, it's hard for me to believe at all. I do not believe every day with Jesus is sweeter than the day before. I think life is hard; sometimes it becomes almost unbearable. In the words of the great song sung by Bonnie Raitt, "To believe in this living is just a hard way to go."[5]

Life is hard, and sometimes God doesn't seem to be there when you need him. Sometimes the ways of God are hard to understand, even harder to follow. When we represent the Christian faith as one long joyride to heaven, we misrepresent the gospel. When life doesn't turn out that way, we undermine the credibility of our faith. Jesus told his disciples to pick up their cross and follow him. Cross-bearing is an essential part of our faith. People know life is hard, and we have to be straight when we tell them about it.

The Good, the Bad, and the Guy with His Hand in the Air

This isn't the only time I have done this. The week I conducted the funeral for the wife of one of my best friends, I said the same thing to the Kairos crowd: "Here is where I am; this is what I'm going through. I know you want to put me on a pedestal and imagine that I'm some kind of a super Christian, but I'm not. I'm just a man. I am just like you, and I have my struggles. Frankly, I do better on some days than others."

I share good times with them as well. Just a few weeks ago, as I was writing this book, my father's birthday fell on a Tuesday. I put my father on speakerphone with them that night. (If you knew my dad, you would know what a great risk this was.) We sang "Happy Birthday" to him. As we hung up, my dad ended the phone call the way he always does.

"Son, I love you, and I am proud of you," he said.

"I'm proud of you, too, Dad. Love you."

It didn't strike me as anything remarkable. That's the way my dad and I end every conversation. But when Kairos ended, I was surrounded by a number of young men. Each one of them had a different version of the same sentiment:

"I would give anything to hear my father tell me he loved me."

"I've never heard my father tell me he was proud of me."

"You're a lucky man, Mike."

I know that using your life as a running sermon illustration carries risks. I don't overuse it. If you come to Kairos regularly, you will see we spend much more time in prayer, worship, and actual Bible study than we do talking about me. Kairos is not about me. I am not special. I'm just a married guy with two kids and a mortgage, trying to figure it out just like you are. And that's the point. Because most of them are new to the faith, they literally do not know what Christianity is supposed to look like. They don't know what prayer looks like, or what it means to forgive or to confess. Someone has to teach them, and the best way to teach them is to model it for them.

Paul wrote to the Philippians, "Whatever you have seen me do, you do" (Phil. 4:9, author paraphrase). I didn't fully understand this passage until I became a father, and I found myself saying to my sons, "Here, let me show you how to do that," or, "Watch me, and then I'll watch you do it on your own." Tying your shoelaces, cleaning your room, using a knife and a fork, balancing a checkbook—all of these life skills that we pass down from generation to generation aren't just talked about in theory. They are demonstrated in real life.

Can you imagine using a PowerPoint slide to explain to children how to tie their shoes? No, you sit down with the children, tie their shoes for them, and then you show them how to do it themselves.

One of my favorite episodes of *The Andy Griffith Show* is the one in which Aunt Bee first comes to live with Andy and Opie. Things don't go well, and Aunt Bee decides to return home. As she's getting on the bus, Opie tells his dad that they can't send Aunt Bee away.

"She's helpless," Opie tells Andy. "She doesn't know how to fish, hit a baseball, or throw one."

Opie has no idea how Aunt Bee is going to make her way in the world.

Those of us who have been in church a long time forget that many of the people we meet in this type of ministry are helpless in matters of applied faith. They are being hit with a lot of different decisions, decisions that will affect them for the rest of their lives. Which job do I take? Do I go back to school? Is it time for me to get married? To this person? On and on the questions come, and they really want to do the right thing. Few people get up in the morning and say to themselves, "Today I'm going to screw my life up beyond all recognition."

Remember, they are making these decisions without any tangible support from a respected older adult. Their parents may have paid for their education, but now these young adults feel like they are on their own. Not only do they feel alone; they still feel angry, and as a result they are not only trying to figure out their own lives, but they are committed that they will "never be like them," whoever "them" may be. They are living against the memory of the person who caused them such pain. A young man will not choose a particular career, despite having a high aptitude for the profession, because that's what dad did. A young woman avoids using a natural talent because "that's what my parents wanted me to do." If the parent liked X, the young adult hates X for no other reason other than that the parent liked it. It's not a decision they've thought through or made intentionally. They're a bundle of quivering emotions, all reaction, no muscle or bone. They're volatile and fragile. Their lives are messy, and they're frustrated because they "should be" able to get it together. It just doesn't seem that simple to them. I relate.

Remember the kid in your class who always had his hand in the air? That was me. In seminary I was always the guy asking the questions that weren't on the syllabus. You know how that guy feels? He feels like a pain in the butt. Everybody wants to stick to the outline, fill in the blanks, check the boxes. Postmoderns don't want to do that. The box doesn't work for them. They are attracted to someone who sees the gray area, who has ragged edges, who has his hand in the air. Postmodern isn't generational. A lot of us over twenty-five still have our hands in the air.

Don't get me wrong; I don't try to be one of them. I'm fifty-one years old; gravity wins. The fact that I'm fifty-one and happily married with two grown sons gives me credibility with them. But so does the fact that I can't draw.

Little Dude

I use a whiteboard when I am teaching, and I can't draw. One night when I was trying to make a point, I drew a stick man, and they named him Little Dude. Little Dude shows up in a lot of theological studies. Little Dude was in the lion's den. They laughed because I couldn't draw lions. I even got on a Web site (yes, there are Web sites to teach you how to draw lions), and I practiced my technique, but I was lousy at it. So I ended up drawing stick lions with wild hair. They were laughing and cheering me on. I drew a really big one with a nasty face. He really had an attitude. They knew what I was trying to communicate: life is ferocious. But drawing stick lions took the edge off.

When we were talking about the theological concept of *imago Dei* (signed by the Creator), it was in the context of the fall. I drew Little Dude up there and then erased his middle. His head was disconnected from his legs. It was a pretty powerful moment when they saw the disconnected human being up there. I had just named their experience.

These kids are having their midlife crisis early. It's called a quarter-life crisis. I admire them; they're braver than I was at their age. They are brave enough to say on the front end, "I don't know anything about how to make life work." This makes learning about Jesus and discipleship extraordinarily practical. Theology matters when it helps them connect their heads to their legs.

Gerald Stow is a guy who understands and embodies this. Gerald is a retired Southern Baptist pastor, a retired denominational executive in his seventies. Currently he's the chairman of trustees of our church. He still speaks the King James English, combs his hair straight back, and sings in a southern gospel quartet, but he loves Kairos kids because they are seekers. He shows up on Tuesdays, walks around, introduces himself to these kids, listens to their stories, prays with them, and loves on them. And they love him because they know he is the real thing.

You may be thinking that you really don't want to live your life this publicly. I certainly understand the need for privacy and the need to protect your family. I'm not encouraging a public voyeurism of faith where you "spiritually undress" in front of these young adults week after week. I am saying this: your life must *validate* your faith walk in every area, or your message will be discounted. You do not have to be perfect, but you do have to be faithful. You will have to be honest even when the honesty is painful. They want to know if Jesus can make a real difference in the real world, and theories won't communicate that kind of truth. You have to tell them about your journey, your lessons, and your witness. Of course, all of this has to be steeped in scriptural truth. People will watch you long before they listen to you. They will learn to trust Jesus in little ways before they will make a big commitment to him. You will have to show them what a committed life looks like before they will take the risk of following. Let's remember that the one thing no one could dismiss about the early disciples was the obvious change Jesus made in their lives.

The early church leaders kept making the same point in their letters: the church must be qualitatively different from the culture around it. Believers must live in such a way that even when they are accused of wrongdoing, their lives will be evidence that makes the charges unbelievable. Our faith has been privatized to the point that we think it is no one else's business, retreating to the false sanctuary of each person's conscience. As a result, people in our culture are no longer sure who is a Christian and who isn't. Recent studies have shown we get divorced at the same rate as the general public, our addiction rates are the same—in short, there is no difference between a Christian's life and the lives of everyone else. Because they don't see us living the truth, they won't listen to the truth we bring. Our lifestyles invalidate our message. I have often reminded my congregation that the world isn't disappointed with us because we are different. They are frustrated with us because we aren't different enough.

When a suicidal gunman attacked an Amish schoolhouse and murdered several students, the world was stunned at the horror of the tragedy, then left speechless by the reaction of the Amish community. Instead of anger and resentment, the Amish community reached out to the family of the gunman, even attending his funeral, because the Bible says you mourn with those who mourn. While the world may not follow the Amish in their simple lifestyle and shunning of technology, they were deeply moved by a faith community that could respond to such tragedy with forgiveness and grace. For just a moment, the world saw how Jesus would respond and was willing to consider a Jesus who could help them deal with the dark side of life.

The Dark Side

Steve waited around after Kairos until everyone had left. He was going through a job transition and money was tight, but those weren't the issues that were bothering him.

"A few weeks ago you said if you can't forgive somebody else, then Jesus won't forgive you. Is that true?"

"Well," I answered, "it's true that holding a grudge against someone else will hinder the Lord from working in your life."

"Then maybe Jesus and I have spoken for the last time," he said.

"Whoa, that's a pretty strong response!" I replied. "What's going on?"

We pulled out some chairs from the nearby table, and he began to tell me the story. He'd been dating a girl that he thought he was going to marry. He'd gone over to her apartment to tell her that he had found a job in Atlanta and was going to be moving. The job paid more money; they would finally be able to get married. That's when she told him that she wouldn't be moving to Atlanta or getting married to him. She was seeing someone else. He found out a lot of things he hadn't known until that moment. He hadn't known she'd gotten pregnant during their relationship or that she had an abortion—all without telling him. Tears welled in his eyes; he twisted his hands together anxiously; and his right leg bounced up and down as if he was trying to throttle back the anger.

"I will never forgive her," he said. "And if Jesus won't talk to me because of that, he'll just have to understand."

"But you're going to have to work through this somehow," I said. "You're going to live to somewhere around ninety years old. Seventy years is a long time to let the anger eat you up."

"But it's just not right!" he protested.

"No, it's not," I agreed. "But that's not the question you're being asked. The question for you is, what are you going to do with what you now know?"

"I'm going to hate her for the rest of my life."

"That's one option, but there may be a better way."

"What?" he asked.

"Forgiveness."

"Never happen."

"Not right away, but it can."

"Do you really believe that?" he asked, looking me in the eye. "I don't even know what forgiveness looks like."

I began to tell him my story. No one lives on this planet without being wounded or betrayed. The question is, how do you live through it? Here's what I have learned. Here's how I dealt with my own anger.

I said from experience, "You'll forgive her when you realize that your healing will have to come from someplace else, from Jesus."

"But he won't talk to me if I won't forgive her."

"Forgiveness is a process, a journey, and if you are being faithful to keep walking, Jesus will walk with you. When your anger at her becomes more important than anything else, well, your whole life freezes up."

"How do I start, Mike?"

"Do you journal? No? Start. Buy yourself any kind of notebook, pick up a pen, and start writing. Trust me, when you put your pen on the paper, the pen will know what to do. Just start writing. Don't worry about how you write, just write. If we're going to walk down this road of forgiveness, the first thing we have to do is know where we are. Get started and keep me posted."

He brought back his journal the next week. We sat down and went over it. Page after page was filled with hurt, grief for dreams that had died, and the loss of the life he had planned. Sometimes he wrote with such anger the pen almost would tear the paper. His handwriting would change from a fairly readable cursive to large, ill-formed letters that looked like they had been written while riding down a bumpy road. Little by little, his questions turned from, "How could she have done this?" to, "What am I going to do now?" Forgiveness is a slow journey. Steve has since moved to Atlanta, and we correspond through e-mail. He hasn't completed his task of forgiveness, but he is still moving down the road toward forgiveness and wholeness.

"I thought Christians were always supposed to be happy," he told me. "No one has ever talked to me the way you have."

"That's what pastors do," I told him, but it made me sad to hear him say that. Too many young people go through their lives without a significant adult who will listen to them. If they do have some kind of encounter with Christ, they often have no one to listen and interpret. For all of the Samuels in the world, we need more Elis.

Ordination

Samuel, the boy who would grow up to be one of the greatest prophets of Israel, was awakened by the call of God. Only Samuel didn't know it was God calling. The third time God called, Eli told Samuel, "Listen because God is speaking." Without Eli how would Samuel have ever known? Surely God can make himself known in any way he chooses, but many times we are used to confirm God's word. God's word to Samuel is confirmed by Eli; God's word to the apostle Paul is confirmed by Annanias. Over and over again, people who have an encounter with the living God have someone sent to help them put it into some kind of context. The world is full of Samuels who have no framework, no worldview that would allow them to recognize God working in their world. Eli knew from his own experience, and that is what he shared with Samuel (see 1 Sam. 3:1–10).

The irony is that young adults want someone to talk with them about these issues, but few people have given evidence that they know Jesus and understand his ways. In the world of televangelists, scandals with religious leaders, and pompous talking heads on roundtable shows, people no longer grant a minister any kind of special authority. You have to be ordained by this congregation of young adults. Every minister is ordained again and again. First a minister has a formal ceremony when the church confirms to the minister, "We have seen the Spirit work in your life, and we are granting you authority to work among us." Then, wherever ministers work, they will be ordained again, as the people to whom they are ministering say to them in some way, "We have watched you long enough to see how God is working in your life, and we will grant you authority to work among us." If you want to work among this demographic, you have to live your life in such a way as to be ordained by them for your ministry.

Journaling:
A Kairos Guided Prayer

Write It Down

Sometimes using more of our senses helps us remember and engage. If you simply come and watch, you don't ever fully engage.

The Bible tells us that the Scriptures are like food. They are like bread. And so we come tonight to eat, to nourish ourselves as believers, as disciples of Christ so we can grow strong in our service to him. I don't know about you, but before I eat I like to wash my hands, especially if you have a job like I do where you shake hands with people all day. By the time you get to dinner, your hands need to be washed. I don't know what's going on in your life right now. I don't know where you are, what kind of day you had. I don't know what kind of life you've had before now. I don't know what brought you here tonight. I know this: before there was a clock to keep time, before the sun started rising and setting, before the earth ever spent one moment spinning in front of the sun, the Lord knew about this moment, this time. He knew you would be here, and the Lord himself has come.

Write down those thoughts, those issues that would keep you from being fully here. It may be, "Call my brother when I get home." Sometimes you have lots of thoughts in your head, and they won't sit still until you write them down. They keep walking around. It could be just a note to yourself. It could be something like, "Here's what I'm angry about," or, "Here's what I'm guilty about; here's what I need to confess." But let's just spend a few moments getting ready, washing our hands, cleansing our hearts and minds so we will be ready to break the bread of worship. So if you need to close your eyes, close your eyes. If you need to keep writing, keep writing. This moment is yours. However you need to get your heart and mind focused in the presence of the risen Lord, you do that now.

God Is Listening

Perhaps you have some big pressure in your life. Maybe you've had a doctor's appointment or a job interview, and this is what's weighing on your heart and mind. You're anxious about starting your next semester of school. You've just gotten your first job. Write it down. Talk honestly to the Father about it. Now, I understand some of you did not have a good relationship with your dad, so when I tell you God loves you like a father, that kind of freaks you out. But understand: Jesus was looking for a metaphor, a word picture, so that you could understand how God feels about you. The best one he could find is the way the perfect father loves his child. The Father waits now for your presence. Come and talk to him the way a child talks to his dad: "Here's what's going on. Here's where I'm hurting. Here's what I need. Here's a friend I'm worried about." Don't worry about making it sound religious. Don't worry about praying right. Just trust him to hear you.

Do you need to use this time for confession? Has someone wronged you? Do you need to forgive?

This is what God says to you: "Seek the Lord while He may be found. Let the wicked man turn from his ways and the evil man turn from his thoughts. For our Lord is quick to forgive, and eager to heal. 'For my ways are not your ways,' says the Lord. 'My thoughts are not your thoughts. For as high as the heaven is above the earth so my ways and my thoughts are above yours. My word does not return to me empty but it accomplishes the purpose for which I spoke it'" (Isa. 55:6–11, author paraphrase).

• • •

Lord, we search for you the way a panting deer looks for water. We know unless we find you, like the animal knows it must find water, we will not stay alive long. Open yourself to us now. Let your love, your grace, and your mercy flow down on us like Niagara Falls until we feel like we are just going to drown in you. Amen.

CHAPTER EIGHT

Evangelism: Confrontation versus Conversation

*W*hen I was growing up in a small mill town church in Huntsville, Alabama, we were serious about evangelism. This was at the height of Billy Graham's crusade successes. People were gathering by the thousands and being saved by the hundreds. Every Christian, especially every Southern Baptist, was expected to be involved in the work of "personal soul-winning." We were expected to be actively engaged in one-on-one evangelism, and we were expecting to see some kind of explosive results. With the conversion of the apostle Paul as our model, we expected bright lights to flash, voices from heaven that would lead to instantaneous and dramatic conversions. We memorized Bible verses, carried around pamphlets, and were always waiting to meet someone who "didn't know Jesus."

We had enough success doing confrontational evangelism that we thought we were doing the right thing the right way. I am not putting anyone down, but any good tool is not right for every job. The longer I stayed with this confrontational approach, I was more and more convinced that there had to be another way to help someone find a relationship with Jesus Christ, mainly because my friends started avoiding me, afraid I would start witnessing to them! "True believers" told me I could expect this; these friends of mine were obviously running from the Lord. I would have to expect to lose some friends if I wanted to live for Jesus. But I had a feeling it was more than that. Some of my friends just got tired of being hustled, even for Jesus. It was like being around a salesman who is always demonstrating his product. It gets old after a while. Sometimes they just wanted to talk about football.

I started looking around for other ways to present the gospel. I found lots of evangelism products, but they all seemed to be based on the same model. You were supposed to memorize Scriptures and then guide the conversation toward certain topics so that you could answer with the verses you had memorized. I wasn't good at it. I could never get people to ask the questions in the order that I had memorized the Scriptures. Besides that, the questions we were supposed to ask were extremely removed from the real concerns of the people I was talking to. I'm glad I memorized all those Scriptures because sometimes when you're in a conversation you have to pull the passage off the top of your head. For this discipline I will always be grateful. Still, I couldn't help but think there had to be a more natural approach to sharing the gospel.

What Would Jesus Do?

To my surprise I found models of a more comfortable approach in the Bible. John 3 records the famous conversation between Jesus and Nicodemus. The first thing I notice is that Nicodemus came to Jesus. That is, Nicodemus initiated the conversation when he was ready to deal with his questions. Jesus was available, but Jesus didn't force the moment. He waited until Nicodemus came to him.

Second, there was no game of verbal chess. Jesus wasn't trying to box Nicodemus into a conversational corner where he would have to confess Jesus was the Savior. Jesus was honest, bluntly so, but he seemed content to let Nicodemus set the pace and deal with the topics that concerned him. Jesus was confident in himself and confident in Nicodemus. Nicodemus was a bright and sincere man, and Jesus was confident that if Nicodemus would trust the process until it came to its natural conclusion, Nicodemus would become a believer. Jesus didn't force the issue. When Nicodemus left, he hadn't yet made a profession of faith. While it does seem that Nicodemus became a believer, Jesus was willing to let the process work over several months or even years. If the light came to Nicodemus, it was the slow dawning of the sunrise, not the blinding ray we are always looking for.

The second story that caught my attention was the story of Jesus healing the blind man, found in Mark 8. Some people find Jesus and bring a blind man to be healed. Jesus takes the man away from the crowd, spits on his eyes, and lays hands on him. When Jesus asks if he can see anything, the blind man answers, "I see men walking around, and they look like trees." He can see but not clearly. Jesus again lays his hands on the man's eyes, and the blind man's eyes are completely healed. What is curious about this process is that the healing is not instantaneous. Jesus has to lay his hands on the man twice. Did Jesus fail when he first tried to heal the man? Did Jesus need a do-over?

Obviously not, but this does bring to our attention that some transactions require more than one step. Sometimes healing and salvation are a process, not an event. They happen in God's own (*kairos*) time. This might be days, months, or even years. While this has always been true, I bring it up because in postmodern America, this seems to be the rule rather than the exception.

The last point I want to bring up in my rather casual perusal of evangelism techniques in the New Testament is Paul's habit of going to the local synagogue when he entered a new city. From that base he would preach Jesus as the Messiah and follow the opportunities as they were presented to him. Paul would go to a place, a safe place of meeting, to make himself available for discussions and theological

debates. I am not saying we need to start hanging out at local syna-
gogues; I am saying that Paul's practice of establishing a public presence where he could be approached by people who wanted to know
more about his message is a practice we need to rediscover in the
local church. We need to practice being approachable. We need to
learn the art of hanging out in public places just to talk.

Is This Seat Saved?

Ministers today are viewed as religious professionals. We have
offices, keep calendars, manage our time, and set goals. In some situations you would be hard pressed to distinguish the pastor of a local
church from bankers, attorneys, or other community professionals.
While this professional understanding of ministry does have some
advantages, a significant disadvantage is that we expect the world to
make an appointment with us, to come by for a one-hour visit while
we diagnose their spiritual needs the way a doctor might diagnose
an illness from the patient's description of symptoms. Most people
will not call a pastor with whom they have no relationship to discuss spiritual matters. People need some point of connection, some
opportunity to meet before the conversation will turn to matters of
salvation.

Sadly ministers are not considered by the general community
as professionals who can do a person much good. Counselors, psy-
chotherapists, psychologists, psychiatrists, or even professional life
coaches are seen as individuals who are more qualified to engage
in a profound spiritual conversation. Even the manager of the local
bookstore who can guide the person to the latest self-help book will
be viewed as more valuable than the average local pastor. I am a local
pastor. I don't mean to put down anyone, but the reality is that in
postmodern America we are no longer granted the measure of public
respect accorded to us by previous generations.

The first step in postmodern evangelism is to get out of the
office and into the community. The first assignment is to create

opportunities for conversations. This is not evangelism; it's more like evangelism research. Local pastors are going to have to understand that we no longer live in a predominately Christian society. Most of the people in our communities are unchurched and relatively uninterested in church. They may respect Jesus, but they don't believe in him as Savior. "If you want to believe, that's fine," your neighbors will say, "but don't try to push it on me." Once your neighbors find out you're a minister, they will begin to keep a polite distance. If you are going to be heard, you will be heard as their friend, not as the pastor of the local church.

You have to get out and coach Little League ball games. You have to serve on community boards. You have to be seen as a person who cares about the community. More than that, you have to be a person who *does* care about the community. This is the place where God wants you to work. This is the mission field he has given to you, and you have to know it better than anyone else. As you do, you will discover community needs your church can meet. In meeting these needs, conversations will start, and relationships will begin to develop. Kairos is involved in "move-in days" at local colleges and universities. We help students get their stuff up to their dorm rooms, and in the process we get to know a lot of people. In Nashville we are one of the sponsors of a local downtown event called Movies in the Park. We set up a booth and give out free water or gadgets with the Kairos logo. People will stop and ask who we are or what we're doing there. We've also been able to establish some key relationships with leaders of the local media because of our community involvement. From time to time, we get a little free airplay because they know us.

And yes, we drink lots of coffee. We drink coffee early in the morning, after lunch, late in the afternoon. We are available on their way into work, after work, midday break, late morning cup of java—any time and any place. I am out so much in local coffee shops, people joke that I have a north office and a south office. They aren't going to come to my office, but they will meet me at Starbucks,

Borders, Barnes & Noble, or anywhere else that has a table and a decent cup of coffee.

We talk. Rather, they talk. I listen. The first requirement of postmodern evangelism is not that you are a good talker but that you are a good listener. In the rush of today's world, the gift of attention is one of the best gifts you can give someone. People don't have time to listen to one another. And while e-mail and texting can be good things, they can't take the place of people who are willing to give you their time. As you listen, you will hear the story of a person who is trying to get by, and wounds sometimes long ignored will begin to surface.

Can You Hear Me?

My major was speech and drama. People always assume that helps me with preaching. It actually helps in pastoral care because I can always keep a straight face no matter what anybody tells me. It's like being able to hold a straight face in the punch line of a comedy. When people tell me something they think is going to shock me, I can control my response. A good listener needs to be unshockable.

The main thing is to pray for those who are talking to you while they are talking to you so the Spirit will help you hear key words or phrases that unlock the doors to their hearts. Most people don't know themselves that well, so you're looking for that phrase that will allow you to ask the next question to get to the heart of the problem. Listening in this way helps them name their pain. It walks them down the road of compassion. Most of them know they have screwed up. They don't need you to remind them. First they need to hear, "I know that was painful for you. Tell me how you're trying to deal with it."

You will begin to love these young adults. People who are involved at Kairos have all had that moment when they walk away from a conversation and find themselves praying, "Please, Jesus, help me find a way to reach these guys." For me, it was one night after a teaching session. I was sitting at my table in the back. Person after person came by and talked to me about what we had said during the night, about their relationships with parents, ex-boyfriends or ex-girlfriends, about betrayal by friends, abuse by bad bosses, and where to find Jesus in all of this. I remember feeling I might drown in the river of pain that had broken through their dams of pretense and washed over all of us there.

"Jesus if you are here," I kept praying, "help me find a way."

No Talk Is Small Talk

I grew up the son of a storyteller. My dad is a fabulous storyteller, and I've always been fascinated with stories and loved to hear people's stories. When you're new in the ministry, you understand preaching as a monologue. You think, *I've studied all week; here's what I have to tell you.* As you grow and mature in your preaching, you understand that it is a dialogue. You have to be able to anticipate and understand the questions your congregation is bringing to the sermon moment in order to be able to preach effectively to them. So you learn to listen to conversations that they don't think are important, the ones in which they tell you what's going on in their lives. You listen throughout the week, and then you work that back into your sermon.

It's the same with these young adults. Everything about them is telling you something. You know, they've got the hat on backwards, tattoos, piercings. People say, "They're just doing that for attention." Absolutely, and for God's sake, let's make sure they get it. Ask them. I've had some fascinating conversations.

"Love the eagle on your forearm. Tell me about it. Did that hurt?"

They always have a story about where they got it and what it means. A tattoo usually marks a significant event in the person's life. "I got it in memory of my grandfather," they'll begin, and you realize that you've been invited to step on sacred ground.

I am constantly surprised by the courage of some of these young adults. They are fighting battles with long odds. More times than not, I end up walking away from these conversations with a profound respect for the integrity with which they are trying to live their lives. If we knew the inner battles of some of these young people, we would stop judging and start praying for them. We would pray hard. The battle is that intense for some of them.

Once they understand you value them, that you're not trying to sell them anything or manipulate them, real honest conversation begins. If you listen to them, they will listen to you. They will ask questions, and you will get the chance to tell them about Jesus. Sometimes they will want to talk about theology, especially if something has been in the news. All of the debate about *The DaVinci Code* gave us a lot of opportunities to have conversations about the real Mary Magdalene and what happened to Jesus after the crucifixion. With the recent publications from the so-called New Atheist, we have more opportunities for conversations about the existence of God and the meaning of life.

For the most part the conversation begins with how you came to know Jesus, how you know Jesus is working in your life. Is what you are saying about Jesus something you have experienced, or is it just something that you have read in a book? In the New Testament the early church talked about the Jesus they had met, what they had seen and heard. Early evangelism was a first-person account of their relationship with Jesus. We are in an era that resembles the situation of the early church—many different religions, many different cultures, hostility toward the message of Jesus—and believers once again have to begin our stories with Jesus as we know him to be firsthand.

Long Walk to Freedom

You can expect these conversations to go on for several weeks. They will listen, drop out for a while, think about what you said, and come back with a list of new questions. During this time they will begin to open up more and more. Don't be surprised if they find themselves in some kind of situation where they will test the teachings of Christ, just to see how true they are in real life. Does prayer work? Does Jesus answer prayers? How do I know? What if I pray for this or that? Will Jesus hear me? Sometimes evangelism and discipleship seem to be the same thing. You end up teaching even while you are trying to persuade.

Patience is the key. You have to be willing to talk to them a long time before you earn their trust. You will walk with them a long way before they will trust you with the secrets they are carrying. Someone they trusted has wounded most of these young adults and, as a result, they are slow to open themselves up again. Understanding this reality will help you understand that the evangelism process may take place over months and involve e-mails, text messages and phone calls, impromptu conversations, and long discussions over coffee. Because of their personal history and the cultural milieu, substantial work in preevangelism has to be done before evangelism can actually begin. When I started in my ministry almost thirty years ago, you would always begin with, "The Bible says." Everyone recognized the Bible as authoritative. That is no longer the case. Your preevangelism has to include a philosophical defense of God's existence, the history of the Bible and its development, and lastly a theory of the atonement that would explain why Jesus had to die and how his death is essential for forgiveness. Then you can talk about a relationship with Jesus.

And then the really hard work starts. We have to adjust our understanding of evangelism to include working with new believers until they become maturing believers. We would call the police on a parent who brought a child home from the hospital just after birth and left that child to grow up on his own. That would be criminal. Yet that is what is done in local churches all the time. People come to Christ; we drop them in the baptistery and run out to win another soul. Far too many of our churches have too small an understanding of evangelism. Being born again means just that—born again. New

Christians have to start all over. They have to learn to walk again, talk again, and think again; and they have to do this while they are unlearning a lifestyle that takes them away from Christ.

At this point a lot of us get frustrated. We think the conversion experience is an instant quick fix, that we are so totally remade in the moment that we will not feel the pain of the previous moment. Jesus spent much time talking about agriculture. An authentic conversion, the remaking of a life into the likeness of Christ takes time. A person cannot microwave discipleship. Seeds have to be planted, watered, and tended; and then in due time, in God's own time, the harvest comes. Too many people try to rush this process and end up with a superficial change rather than a soul-deep transformation.

To most of us, the word *repent* means to apologize for some past action. The word literally means "to turn around." The person is going one way, stops, turns around, and starts walking in a different direction. Most people understand repentance to mean you get a clean slate through forgiveness. You do, but you are still in the same place, although now walking in a different direction. If you are converted in rehab, you are still in rehab. Your spot on the GPS doesn't change.

Let me give you an example. Let's say I am taking I-40 West from Nashville. Now, if I leave Nashville on I-40 West, I'm going to Memphis. But what if I don't want to go to Memphis? Then I have to pull off at the nearest exit and turn around. I have to get on I-40 East back to Nashville. That's repentance. Notice, just because I've repented, my position doesn't immediately change. I am still some miles away from Nashville. My position will gradually improve, but only as I keep driving. Too many of us, to stay with this analogy, think conversion means Jesus grabs us and throws us back into Nashville. He rarely does that. People find they still have cravings, pain, and the same wounds. They are walking in a new direction, but they still have to keep walking. They have to walk past the wreckage of their old lives, their bad habits, and wrong turns. Many people find this to be frustrating. Some give up when they realize this. We must help new Christians understand that the healing is in the journey. There are no shortcuts, no quick fixes. Becoming more Christlike is putting one foot in front of the other for the rest of your life.

The Right to Speak

I do not want to leave the impression that we have any real choice in trying to reach this generation. These young adults are in every community, every suburb, every ethnic group, and every socioeconomic group. The church is called to reach those who need to know Christ. This mission field is in your local colleges, universities, coffee shops, bookstores, and factories. Anywhere young adults gather—that's a mission field, a mission field that must be reached.

As in any mission field, you have to analyze needs and opportunities. You have to learn to understand the culture, to speak the language of the culture. This is a different group. You may just be going across the street to reach them, but you are crossing a huge cultural chasm as wide as the Pacific Ocean.

Like any people group, one size will not fit all. Your strategy will be unique to your situation and with your people. But make no mistake, we have no other option than to spend our lives—everything we are and have—to reach these young adults.

Repenting:
A Kairos Guided Prayer

Relax

Get comfortable; close your eyes. We come to this prayer time, and I don't want you to be looking around, worried about anybody else. I want you just to be dealing with your own stuff.

Release

A lot of stuff we have talked about tonight is pretty heavy, difficult, complex. I want us all to begin with a kind of confession but not confessing what you may think. I want us to confess, men and women alike, that we have falsely allowed our ideas of beauty, our ideas of love, our ideas of intimacy to be defined by a sick culture. I'm going to repent that I've allowed my ideal of beauty to be infected by a sick culture. I'm going to release those false images. I'm going to repent of those false standards, and I'm going to confess that God made me beautiful. God made me beautiful. Say that out loud: "God made me beautiful."

God did not create you and step back and say, "I didn't do well there." The story says he created me and said, "This is good."

"God made me beautiful." Confess it. The only standards of beauty we care about, the only standards of love, the only standards of relationship, are those that belong to the kingdom, not to this culture.

Repent

Let me talk to the guys a little bit. Don't play with this, guys. This is dangerous. It is a fire that will scar your soul to the point of your not being able to feel love when it comes. If you are tempted here, stop. If you struggle with it, confess it right now: "Dear Lord, you know I have this problem." As you confess it, confess the wound that drives you to it: "Dear Lord, you know how I feel about myself. You know the problem I have with my image. You know how lonesome I am. You know how afraid I am." Confess that underlying wound that drives you to this.

Reach Out

This next step is going to be a little scary, but it has to happen. You need to find somebody to talk to. I'll be at the back. Aaron and some other guys are there. You find a guy to talk to. You've got a guy in your small group, a guy at your table. That's fine. You talk wherever you are comfortable, and you say, "I think I have this problem. This is what I'm dealing with. I want you to pray with me. I want you to hold me accountable. I want you to be my brother through this." The worst thing you can do is walk out of here and say, "I don't have a real problem. I don't have anything going on." You think you can handle this thing by yourself. You cannot.

If a friend reaches out to you in confession, do not condemn him, do not put him down. He is taking an incredible risk. Respect the trust he is giving to you.

Ladies, confess that you have allowed a culture to wrongly define beauty in your life. Understand that you were created gloriously in the image of God. Do not sell what is treasure as if it were junk. You're not junk. And if this is an issue that is going on in your life in any way, confess it. Find a friend and talk about it. Find someone to hold you accountable. Deal with it. Women in the back want to talk with you, want to be your friend. If you're not careful, you'll become so suspicious, so cynical that you won't trust love when it comes.

If you choose to be married, if it is God's plan for you to be in love, then I pray for you the same regret that I have. Yes, regret. In June, Jeannie and I will celebrate twenty-seven years of marriage. I regret that I was engaged for ten months. I should have married her faster. I want you to find me at the nursing home where I'll be when you're celebrating your twenty-seventh anniversary. I want you to walk up to me and say, "You know, we made the same mistake. We should have gotten married sooner. We're so crazy about each other." I want that for you. But you won't get there unless you can tell the real thing from the false thing.

Like I said earlier, it all starts with a relationship with Jesus Christ and knowing who you are in him. And that may be brand-new news to you. If it is, I'll be glad to talk with you. I'll be hanging around the back.

Respond

The rest of the time is yours. I don't know what you need to do. You may need to pray with somebody who is sitting near you. You may need to talk with somebody who's around you. You may need to get up and find a person you know is here. Have the conversation; pray together. You may need to find me or one of the other ministers back there. You may need to sit in your chair and quietly write in your journal or just make a note to yourself: "These are some things that are going to be different." You may just want to listen quietly to the worship. You may want to participate.

Kairos is over now. You can do whatever you feel like you need to do. If you need to go, blessings to you. Go safely. We give you this time now to deal with who you are in Christ, and know the treasure that you are and how richly and deeply you are loved.

● ● ●

Jesus, help my friends. Amen.

CHAPTER NINE

Mission before Relief

Robert wanted to go on a mission trip to New York City. He had worked on some community service projects while in college and through his work. He'd enjoyed building a house for Habitat for Humanity and serving in the downtown shelter for the homeless. Robert was a good guy. Everyone around Kairos liked him. So when he signed up to go on the mission trip, no one thought too much about it—that is, until one of his friends told us that Robert was not a believer.

Not a believer?

The friend said Robert had talked about it before, but he had never made the decision to become a follower of Christ. He had never been baptized.

But Robert wanted to go on a mission trip.

Kairos was sending a group of about thirty young adults to work with local churches in inner-city New York. The project planned for this particular year was to paint the neglected rooms of the schools in the communities where our partner churches were ministering.

Robert was a hard worker. Enthusiastic and dependable, he would have made an excellent member of the team. But he had never made a profession of faith.

We had never said that in order to go on this mission trip, you had to be a Christian. (Now, come on, you wouldn't have thought about announcing it either.) What were we going to do?

Before Belief

Anyone who's ever been on a mission trip knows that even though the main objective of a particular trip may not be evangelism, evangelism *always* comes up. It may be during a meal or a work break, but sooner or later someone is going to ask, "Why are you here?" That will give you the chance to say, "We believe that this is what Jesus wants us to do," and from there you will have the opportunity to tell someone else about your faith.

To be honest, we'd never faced this dilemma before. We didn't have a policy. We knew that going on this mission trip would be a good opportunity for these young adults to give something back and do some good team-building. We had just assumed (wrongly) that anyone who would want to pay their way to New York, work in an unair-conditioned classroom with the windows nailed shut, and sleep in a nearby college dorm room would *have* to be a Christian. I don't think that in my entire years of ministry I'd ever had a non-Christian who wanted to go on a Christian mission trip. This one had to be handled carefully. Most of the Kairos team knew Robert and considered him a friend. We needed to be sure we had talked through this one.

We called the leadership of Kairos together. As we presented the situation for their input, some of the team gave the predictable answers.

"Only a Christian needs to go."

"What's he going to say when someone asks him about Jesus?"

"We just need to tell Robert he can't go unless he becomes a Christian."

Others thought that might seem heavy-handed, that Robert would receive it as a threat and not make a decision at all. That wasn't what we wanted, was it?

But then the conversation began to take another turn.

"Who says that the lost ones we're sent to reach have to live in New York?" one of the young people in the group asked. "Couldn't this mission trip be the chance we have to reach Robert?"

Another person pointed out that the disciples weren't instant believers; they had to walk with Jesus for a little while before they got it.

"Maybe Robert is like one of them, and he just has to walk along before he can be sure."

Another one said, "Maybe he needs to see Jesus in a different way."

Not all who hear are convinced to believe just because they hear the Bible stories told to them. Maybe they actually need to see Jesus do something in real life. So that's where we ended up. The decision was made to take Robert. A few of the others were assigned to be his "buddies," like at youth camp, and stick with him.

Robert went on the mission team. He came to the group meetings where we laid out specific conditions for participation. We tried not to assume anything. There were rules about no drinking, no use of inappropriate language, no use of tobacco products, the responsibility to keep curfew and abide by all rules, and so on. Robert eagerly agreed to every one of these expectations. And he kept every one of them. He worked hard, and in the process of seeing what Jesus does all the time on these mission trips, Robert came back a believer.

We asked Robert why he finally made his decision. Was it the meeting with the principal when she told us about the kids who would be in the rooms we painted—how this would make all the difference for these kids who didn't get many breaks? Was it the believers on the trip with him? The worship times? He said it was none of these things. One day, rolling paint on a wall, he realized that there was someone else here besides his team. There was a Presence. Someone was with him. When the team had dismissed to go to bed, he had sat up and prayed. That's when Robert had become a Christian.

Seeing before Believing

One of the things that makes this generation different from others is that they have to see to believe. They are visual. If something is to be real, they have to see it to trust it. That's one of the downsides of growing up with television. The Lord may have blessed those who could believe without being able to see, but he certainly didn't condemn Thomas for wanting to be sure. We have a generation who, like Thomas, want to touch and feel, to see for themselves before they will accept belief as true.

We have to admit, part of this is our fault. As our critics have told us, we're so heavenly minded that we are no earthly good. We sing about heaven, and we talk about loving one another while we ignore the needs of our neighbors and fail to address the injustices that keep so many of our brothers and sisters enslaved. Our evangelistic fervor told us that the most important thing we could do was to reach the person with the message of Christ. The apocalyptic times we were living in, when the Cold War was at its hottest, meant we only had so much time. The preaching of the gospel was more important than programs to feed the hungry, alleviate substandard housing, prevent or treat disease, and improve education. As a result, churches were regarded as irrelevant to the real issues of people's lives. People stopped listening to the message because they saw no real ministry. This has been a major change in the work of the local church during my career. When I was beginning in ministry, you would open your Bible, and that's where the conversations began. Now no one will listen until they see the work you are doing. When someone sees you putting a roof on a house, taking clothes to the homeless shelter, providing neighborhood tutoring, they want to know what you are doing there. Only then can you tell them that your relationship with Christ compels you to show your love for others in real and tangible ways. This is counterintuitive to most churches I know and certainly feels backward to most preachers I know, including me. Our first inclination is to speak then act, but if we continue to do that and not recognize the change in the culture, we will be pushed farther and farther to the margins of the cultural conversation.

Let's be honest, who does this better than the church? In the aftermath of Katrina, churches responded faster and more effectively than the federal government. In many situations we are still engaged in a lot of different places that were affected. We feed the hungry and work with the homeless to restore to them the dignity of a working skill. We teach English as a second language and tutor at-risk kids. The list could literally go on and on. My point is not to provide a comprehensive list of mission and ministry opportunities but to help us understand that what the culture is looking for is a natural strength of the local church. Where else can you find an organized group of volunteers with the necessary skills to provide the services required? Once churches grab hold of this strength, communities will respond, and young adults will be at the front of that line.

For too long there has been a misleading gap between works and faith. While works certainly cannot earn salvation, too many of us took that doctrine to the erroneous conclusion that good works have nothing to do with an authentic faith. Good works are a natural consequence of an authentic faith the way an apple naturally grows on an apple tree. If the roots and trunk are healthy, the apple will grow. If the faith is healthy, the natural expression will be acts of love toward our neighbors. Without good works, the world has a good reason to doubt our faith.

Answering the Pagan

On the other hand, when we focus on good works, when we focus on serving Christ by serving the least of these around us, no one does it better than the church. The church was at the center of the Civil Rights Movement. The church was at the center of the world hunger ministry. As I remind my atheist friends, why is it that you never see an atheist tent at a disaster site? It's always the church that shows up. Why are there no atheist hospitals? The simple answer is that the church is compelled by its love of Christ to care for those people who cannot, for whatever reason, care for themselves. This gives us a tremendous advantage in the war of worldviews. The true church takes the parable of the "least of these" seriously.

Religion may have little authority these days. The Bible may not be considered authoritative. The professional minister may not have authority, but ministry does. They don't listen to what we say, but they do watch what we do. They notice how we walk the walk. Is the church making a difference in the lives of the people in the community?

I call this "answering the pagan." He's the guy who stands up in all the city council meetings and complains that the churches aren't paying taxes, that they take all of the best land in town, but they don't contribute to the community. We have to be able to step up and say, "Here are the things we are doing; here are the reasons our church is a good part of the community. We provide free tutoring. We're involved in repairing substandard housing. We feed the hungry. We take care of the homeless. We rehabilitate senior citizens." And on and on it goes. These hands-on projects are where young adults will learn about faith, about what matters in life, and about what the love of Jesus looks like when it is lived out. They learn about themselves and how Jesus can use them. They learn that they have value beyond their jobs or their income or social status. Young adults want to make a difference. And it makes a real difference in somebody's life that their front porch has been repaired or that the roof doesn't leak anymore. It makes a difference when a woman who is coming off unemployment has a nice dress to wear to her first job interview, that she's had someone sit down with her and help her prepare her résumé in a professional way.

It also makes a real difference to hear somebody say to one of these young adults, "You did a good job." Some of these kids have been told, "You are the bad kid in class. You're the troublemaker." If you can take them out of the buttoned-down school/corporate culture and put them into a Katrina site or an orphanage in Eastern Europe, then you give them a chance to be somebody else. It's similar to what we do with our student ministries. They have yet to be emotionally or spiritually mature enough to do this, but they often rise to the occasion. Often, it's the "troublemaker" or "outsider" who makes the strongest connection on the mission field. He will come back from that place and be the strongest advocate for the outcast, the oppressed, or the disenfranchised.

You don't ever stop trying to reach these kids simply because you're going on a mission trip. To do this is to assume we send only people who already have it all together. Often what God does in us on the mission field is just as important as what he does in those to whom we've been sent. God put a kid on your team because this is the unique moment he's chosen to reach them or teach them. He'll do it in this great journey of discomfort, different smells, and different languages.

Learning Labs

When I was in college, certain classes had laboratories. You would attend a couple of hours of lecture every week, and then you would go to a lab where you would test the theories that you had learned in class. If you studied about a certain species of plant in the textbook, you would go to the lab that afternoon and study that plant in real life. If you heard a lecture about certain chemicals, you went to a lab and experimented with those chemicals so that you could see how they reacted in real life. For every lecture in theory, we had a lab to see how the theory worked in real life. Missions are the labs of our faith. They're where we test and prove what we have been talking about in our worship services, where we learn what the love of Jesus looks like when it is lived out. Missions are where we learn that Jesus cares about those who are in prison, who are hungry, who need clothing, and who are wounded, broken, and washed ashore by the storms of life. When missions are done and done well, the message of Jesus is authenticated in real-life situations, and the ministry is granted permission to speak to the world because the truth has been tested and proved in real life.

Kairos has taken some criticism because we don't take up a regular offering. When you ask these kids to give, they will respond. Tell them orphans in Moldova need socks, and they'll show up next week with ten pairs of socks. But give to an institution or a budget? They're not there yet. They're more likely to send their money to Bono or Jars of Clay's Blood Water Mission. The institution of the church hasn't earned their trust. We can get our feelings hurt about that, or we can find ways to earn it. We'll move toward giving but not right now. Why? Because everybody is after their money. Everything they see at church is about giving money. When they have a significant encounter, they start giving. They may start giving to Kairos. "This is important to me. I want to support it." So their gifts go directly to Kairos and not to the church.

In addition to growing them in the area of giving to this ministry, we need to grow them in the whole area of financial responsibility. Life skills, managing money, and tithing are part of that. We have a lot of response when we deal with basic life skills such as how to balance a checkbook or how to do a budget. One of the weekends we have planned is a life skills workshop. We have friends who are bankers and financial planners coming in to tell them, "Here are the questions you need to ask now that you're twenty-something and starting your life." It will be a Saturday brunch for a couple of hours. Moms and dads didn't teach them these skills. "If I don't have a balanced checkbook, how am I going to tithe? How am I going to understand how God is working in my life if I'm constantly frantic twenty-nine days of the month, wondering how I'm going to pay rent or my car payment?" Before we can teach them to give, we explore stewardship, management, and responsibility that a lot of them haven't learned.

These kids may have several thousand dollars of debt—credit cards, student loans, car payments, all the stuff. They know their financial success may not get better for them as it did for their parents, so they are making different choices about success and what it means. A lot of them are not interested in working their way up the corporate ladder. A job pays the bills and allows them to do the things they want to do, but it doesn't define them. They don't want to have their lives consumed with work as their fathers' were. They want to do something that will make some real and tangible difference. They don't think they can necessarily influence the people with whom they work. They think, *I go and do this job for a few hours. I get what I need. Then I'll come back and hang around the people I can influence.*

A mission trip is where they learn that they can and do have influence. It's where they discover a reason to get out of debt, to be freer to give, to be available to go. One of the members of our original Kairos leadership team, Jen Gash, resigned her job as assistant to Nashville's mayor and formed a not-for-profit ministry called Sweet Sleep that provides beds, mentors, and life skills for orphans in Moldova. Another Kairos member, Jacqueline Schwartz, quit her corporate job, sold her home and her belongings so that she could be free to follow a dream God placed in her heart: taking doctors into Guatemala on medical mission trips. That dream is a full-fledged ministry called The Shalom Foundation. Jen and Jacqueline are examples who remind us that our goal is not to do mission projects but to teach missional living.

This is a great, yet unclaimed, opportunity for the local church. Twentysomethings who have no idea what to do with their lives are not a problem; they are, as Bill and Gloria Gaither put it, great big possibilities. God has given us this unique moment in time to speak into their lives and say, "You can matter for the kingdom. You can be a voice to your culture. People will listen to you speak."

I do not want to give you the impression that you can go out and get people involved in a housing project and everything will change for the better. It doesn't always work, and it doesn't always work cleanly or smoothly. Mission work, like life itself, is messy and frustrating. Not every nonbeliever is going to make a profession of faith. That's the risk you take. Some who claim to be leaders will turn out not to be leaders at all. They will make the same mistakes over and over again, but they are baby Christians, and they're learning how to live the love of Jesus in a hostile and broken world. They're learning. Nothing helps them learn more than experience, knowing you don't have enough money to buy the bricks you need and then all of a sudden having that money appear. Or knowing that no one on your team knows how to lay linoleum, only to find somebody who knows somebody who will come and help you on this project. Over and over again prayers that are prayed, sometimes whispered, are answered in miraculous ways. They learn that Jesus makes a difference in their daily lives, and these lessons are taken from the mission trip back to their offices, homes, and classrooms. They learn to live in what I call the "Divine Maybe." When you realize Jesus has helped you in a previous situation and you are looking at your current situation, you begin to live in the moment of divine possibilities.

"Jesus, you helped me in that moment," you pray. "Help me now."

First-century discipleship was rarely about knowledge. The modern church has made discipleship about information. You go to discipleship classes, and you study. You fill in the blanks in the outline. When you finish that study, you move on to another. Jesus sent the first disciples out on their first mission trip only a few months into the process. He threw them out there, and when they came back, they understood and knew God at a new level—something you can only know by experience.

We would probably not send a Kairos team to a suburb of Portland, conducting door-to-door surveys to help start a church. We would send them to New Orleans or Houston to work with a church doing medical evaluation or children's ministry. They've been to New York, Brazil, India, and South America as part of churchwide teams. It's good for Kairos kids to be with mature believers, and it's really good for mature believers to see these young people coming along. It's good for moderns to see that everything can't be solved with a strategy or an outline. Postmoderns are more comfortable with the ambiguities and messiness of life; they can teach us how to be spontaneous, creative, and intuitive.

A Way That Makes Sense

Community happens when people work together. People who get thrown together on a mission trip, who would never encounter one another in the normal routines of their days, form friend-ships. A senior adult will teach a young person how to square the studs as they are framing a house. On their break young adults will teach senior adults how to use the text feature on their cell phones. Nothing bonds people together like sweat. Nothing pulls them closer together than looking at a problem and solving it together with the combined gifts of the team. Or the moment when the group prays because there is no human solution to the problem they are facing and God provides in such a way that the entire team knows it was from God. Those are the kinds of moments that make you friends for life.

And then there are the conversations. Mission projects give people time to talk. People who wouldn't necessarily think others are interested in what they would have to say can end up talking for hours. These conversations happen over meals, during breaks, and while they are working. Questions about where people came from and where they work lead to questions about life and meaning. In all of that, stories about answered prayers, the faithfulness of Christ in real life, are told and heard, passing from one generation to the next. It's the way the church has grown for two thousand years. Postmodern America is forcing us to rediscover the basics of church life. One of those basics is the natural conversation that happens when people work together. Most people do not sit down and think through their worldview in one discussion. Most of us meander through the difficulties of the essence and meaning of life. We don't go from Roman numeral one through a logical outline of rational thought. We talk a little and then go off and think about what we have learned.

For some, it's the first time they will hear somebody say, "I'm proud of you." It's the first time they will be valued for themselves. From that moment they will begin to understand that this is the way the Lord feels about them. They'll begin to change and see themselves in a different way. They begin to see themselves as persons of value, people who are treasured, people who matter.

Faith can be born on a mission trip. That's what happened to Robert. Faith can grow on a mission trip. That's what happens to most of us. We are all born again in some way. In the learning lab we find Jesus for ourselves—not so much the Jesus of the corporate church or of professional clergy but Jesus who walked around the shores of Galilee and reached out to the poor. We open our lives to the possibilities that God is working in us and around us. We see ourselves in an entirely different light, and it will all start because we see the love of Jesus in real life in a way that made sense. In post-modern America, ministry comes before belief.

One of my favorite groups is an old blues band called the Amazing Rhythm Aces. They have a song about a couple breaking up called "Everybody's Talked Too Much."

This generation believes the church has talked too much and done too little. People have stopped listening. When they see us actually doing something—making a difference in a real way in our communities and the lives of their friends—they'll begin to listen to what we say. Only then will they hear us. Only then will they believe.

Fat Tuesday:
A Kairos Guided Prayer

Give It Up

How many of you know what Fat Tuesday is? Any of you from New Orleans? Fat Tuesday is the day before Ash Wednesday. Ash Wednesday is tomorrow, and it begins the forty-day period before Easter that is traditionally called Lent. It's the time Christians across the generations have selected to be a season of sacrifice, of fasting, to try to enter into Jesus' last days of his journey on Earth. Traditionally, we have given up something. You'll hear people say, "Well, I gave it up for Lent." You give up chocolates, or you give up cheese for Lent. You give up something to make you think about this significant time in the church year. Fat Tuesday is the day before the fasting starts, so traditionally it is a time of gorging and revelry, and you eat all the chocolate or cheese you can today because tomorrow is the beginning of the fast. You do all of that today for tomorrow.

I want us to come to a prayer time of fasting. And I want us to do the most difficult thing of all. I want us to come to a time when we fast from ourselves. We're going to have a prayer time, and we're not going to talk about you at all. I know you're thinking, *What do I talk to Jesus about if I don't talk about me?* In the words of Toby Keith, "I wanna talk about me!"[6] Just think about it. It will come to you in a minute.

Focus

Close your eyes and get in a comfortable position. Most of the time that means both legs on the floor. I don't want your legs crossed so that your feet go to sleep. Just get comfortable. The reason I want you to close your eyes is so that you can focus on being alone. I don't want you to watch anybody. There is a candle on the table. You may want to focus on the candle. Sometimes that is helpful in a time of meditation and prayer. It will remind you that Jesus is the Light of the world.

Let Go

Deep breath in, deep breath out. We start just by taking a few minutes to get here. Most of us start the day running, and we end the day running, and rarely are we ever congruent during the day. That means our mind is at the last meeting we were in or in the middle of our last conversation, or anticipating a conversation we are about to have. But it's rarely with our body at the same time. That's why you hear some spiritual teachers saying, "Be mindful of the moment."

Tomorrow is not here yet. Jesus warned that tomorrow has enough trouble of its own. You don't need to borrow worry. Today is past. Nothing you can do can get it back. All you have is now. This moment, this place, and this time.

Let God

Let's begin with just an outlandish statement of faith. Jesus said, "Consider the sparrows. They give no thought to their life, yet not one of them falls from heaven without your father in heaven knowing about it" (Matt. 10:29–31, author paraphrase). Sparrows are sold for pennies in the market. Surely you're worth more than sparrows.

Think about the lilies of the field. They do not plant crops, they do not harvest crops, and they do not work. Yet Jesus said, "Solomon in all of his glory, could not match the beauty of one of these flowers" (Matt. 6:28–31, author paraphrase). They bloom for a day and wilt tomorrow. Surely you're worth more than lilies.

Then Jesus said, "Give no thought to what you will eat, what you will drink or what you will wear. Pagans consume their time worrying about such things. But as for you, the Father knows you have need of that" (Matt. 6:25–34, author paraphrase). However you need to, for whatever thing in your life you need to express this, thank God. Give praise to the Father for meeting needs before you even know you have them. Confess your faith, your confidence, your trust that he is going to take care of you, no matter what, no matter how big the "what if?" is in your life right now. Some of you are between jobs. Some of you have just graduated and are looking for jobs. Some of you don't like your job, and some of you are changing majors again. That's OK. You need to express to Jesus the confidence you have that he will meet your needs no matter what—your rent, your house payment, groceries, clothes. Pagans worry about such things. Not you.

Get into Goodness

Taking care of that detail frees us up to do some interesting things in this prayer time, like offer your praise to God. Praise him for no other reason than that he and he alone is God. Isn't that good news? You don't have to choose between the top two or three. You don't have to worry about choosing the wrong God and ending up on the wrong side. There's just one. Everything else is make-believe. The Lord your God is one. Praise him for being Creator, for being the Sustainer of life, for being Redeemer, for being Father, for being merciful. Praise him for being who he is.

Let your praise bring you now into thanksgiving. Give thanks to God for what he has done. Pray specifically. Be mindful of his goodness to you.

This past Sunday we celebrated Chris and Craig's twenty-third birthday, and we all went out to lunch. I am sitting next to my wife of almost twenty-seven years, looking at my sons, who are twenty-three, and it seemed like yesterday that I was holding them for the first time. I found myself just watching, trying to hold on to that moment in my head for as long as I could. And I was grateful.

Where in your life have you been intensely aware of the Lord's action? Give thanks.

Get into the Possibilities

Let your thanksgiving now lead you to boldness in prayer. Let's pray huge. Let's pray for something outrageous. Let's pray for the brothers and sisters of the persecuted church. Let's pray for our brothers and sisters in Indonesia who meet under death threats, for the Christians in certain parts of India who are undergoing persecution. Pray for our brothers and sisters in Saudi Arabia, where sharing the gospel will mean the death sentence. Pray for friends you know who are in tough situations. Maybe they are the only Christians in their organization; and maybe, instead of persecution, they are picked on, constantly ridiculed. Pray for your friends who do not know Jesus.

Pray for Kairos, that we will hit the target that Jesus wants us to hit. Now are you feeling bold? Feeling good? Here's the last thing I want you to pray. Tell Jesus, in whatever way you need to, that your life and everything you have is totally available to him and you're ready now to do whatever he needs you to do. Our prayers are always filled with stuff we want Jesus to do. What does Jesus want you to do?

• • •

Our Father, we live in a world that changes from moment to moment. The foundations shift, and the supporting columns topple over. The philosophers point to great truths that do not last. Our friends grab on to fads that fade like the colors of a sunset. We keep looking for a solid place to put our feet down, a rock we can stand on, a rock we can build our lives on. So hear now from a grateful people who have found you to be that rock. And yes, the storms still come, the winds blow, and the rain pelts us, but our little house stands because we built on the rock that you are. So we pray now, Father, that as we close this time of prayer we do so in the confidence that you have heard us and answered us. And now we will worship you in the sure confidence that what you have started you are now completing. And we pray this in your name. Amen.

CHAPTER TEN

Macedonia Isn't That Far Away

I live in two different worlds. In one world I am the senior pastor of Brentwood Baptist Church, a modern multifaceted suburban megachurch. In the other world I am "Uncle Mikey," the teaching pastor of Kairos, a postmodern urban young adult-targeted worship and discipleship experience. On Sunday morning I wear a coat and tie and preach after the offertory. When the sermon is over, I go to the parlor of our church and counsel with people who want to make decisions. On Tuesday night I wear my jeans and teach from the floor using a whiteboard projected onto the screens around Wilson Hall. When the teaching time is over, I sit on a couch in one corner of the room and wait for the young adults to come and talk to me. This is one of the things that makes Kairos unique. We are part of Brentwood Baptist Church and generously supported by the congregation, but in other ways Kairos has become its own church with its own character and style. We are now in the habit of turning down an idea because "it's not Kairos." Most of the time this arrangement works pretty well, but sometimes I find myself caught in the crossfire of expectations and cultures. When it gets confusing, I get to be the interpreter between the two worlds.

The two groups say many of the same things, but they do not speak the same language. Sometimes the conversations remind me of the way parents and teenagers talk to each other, each claiming the other doesn't understand the real world and each being right in their own way. Parents, for the most part, do not understand the world of the teenager; teenagers, despite their worldliness, do not understand the world of their parents. Yet when either takes the time to sit down and listen to the other, they usually find they are dealing with common problems in different contexts. This is true of the parent church and the postmodern church. We are caught in a conflict, but I believe our differences are primarily about context, not content.

Seismic Shifts

The world we live in is changing. It is changing rapidly, and it is changing into a place that no one has ever lived in before. For the first time in history, parents cannot prepare their children for the future. The world their children will inherit will not resemble in any way the world the parents have known.

Recently the earth itself has been profoundly altered. Hurricane Katrina changed the Louisiana delta forever. In New Orleans and the surrounding areas, landmarks have been swept away and will never be rebuilt. Katrina's powerful winds and floods erased several small communities along the coast in Alabama, Mississippi, and Louisiana. These communities are gone. A powerful tsunami was caught on video as it pushed ashore in Indonesia, leveling everything in its path. Entire villages will never be replaced. In the same way our young adults have entered a world where all of the familiar landmarks and road signs have been swept away by this great tsunami of cultural change. What their parents told them was there simply isn't there anymore. A college degree used to be necessary for a good job. Now entrepreneurs challenge the corporate landscape. And the good jobs college students were supposed to get? They're being outsourced to India or China. The giant companies their parents worked for have been bought out or gone out of business. While the work life of the parent may have been numbing in its boredom and sameness, the work life of the young adult is numbing in its uncertainty and confusion.

And what is truth? Most major Christian denominations have dealt with or are dealing with controversy surrounding the authority of the Bible. How literally is the reader to interpret the Bible? Is it authoritative? Is it central to living? Young adults have grown up and are now living in a volatile spiritual environment. As I write these pages, Oprah Winfrey is teaching the content of a New Age bestseller she recently endorsed on her television show. To date, there have been more than ten million downloads of her Internet classroom.

On her first day at work, my research and writing assistant ordered a subscription to *O* magazine in my name!

"Everyone in your congregation watches her show," she said. "You need to know what she's telling them. Like it or not, Oprah is their priest and pastor."

So is Dr. Phil. And Tom Cruise.

Young adults are swimming in a sea of truth, and they've been told they can build their own rafts. Your truth is your truth; my truth is my truth, and it's just as valid (even though the two may be mutually exclusive). All truth is the same. The result is that most young adults have pieced together a worldview from several different sources. They will cobble together this life raft and cling to it until it no longer keeps them afloat. When it crashes, they will simply look around, grab what they need from what is being offered, and build another one. In a tsunami consistency isn't an issue; survival is.

To borrow a word from "old-time religion," they need to be saved. This rescue demands that we strip away the cultural wardrobe we have draped around Christianity and present the gospel in its simplest form. Who says we have to have church on Sunday? Who says it has to be at 11:00 a.m.? Why do I have to wear a suit to church? All of these are culturally, not biblically, imposed. If it is not foundational to the faith, then it is rejected as cultural baggage. If you can prove something useful, then they will make it part of their life, but you must prove its value. For instance, some of our young adults don't like hymns because they've never sung them or heard them. But let one of our senior adults tell the young adult why the hymn is important, and the young adult will sing the hymn with great conviction and enthusiasm. It has been tested in real life. Here is something the older generation and the new have in common: the value of testimony is back. We must learn to tell our stories. What worked in the first century works in the twenty-first century. We must tell them about what we have seen and heard, and we must find a way to tell them in a language they understand.

Going digital means the young adults of Kairos live in the constant state of "now." Texts, e-mails, Internet videos—all in sound bites and snippets of information typed using the symbols of text (c u l8r)—mean information moves swiftly and superficially in their lives. Something that happened this morning can be considered "yesterday" by lunch; by then it will have been discussed and dismissed by all concerned parties. So how do we communicate with a demographic that is moving this fast? You have to be able to say a lot in two- to three-minute sound bites. You have to have your material online and ready to download 24–7. Kairos podcasts are crucial to our success. If they're not ready for download immediately, we hear about it. They don't live on your time clock. Expect e-mails, texts, and downloads from midnight to three in the morning. That's when they're thinking about God. More and more the digital world is where they live. In social networks, gaming, entertainment, and even the workplace—everything in their world is online. If we're going to disciple them, we must find ways that are personal and portable.

What to Expect

One obvious impact of these young adults on the future of the local church is in the area of membership. Membership in an organization isn't important to postmoderns. Young adults run in small and shifting groups called tribes. The central core seems to stay the same, but other friends will come and go over time. The book *Urban Tribes* describes this fluid network, more organism than organization, as the major form of social connecting for young adults. Once the tribe is formed, it moves at will throughout the community. Restaurants, entertainment venues, shopping malls, and a few churches will host the tribe for a while. Then the tribe will move on.

We're going to have to redefine what it means to be a member of the local church. For years it has meant that I can walk down the aisle, sign a form, and never have to come back again, except at Christmas and Easter. If I tithe, I more likely consider it paying dues than stewardship. The expectation was: "I'm on the roll. I'm a club member. And I have all the full rights as member. If my daughter wants to get married in that church, I'm a member. I'd better get the Saturday night that I want. When I'm in the hospital, you'd better come visit me. I'm a member. When I die, I expect to have my funeral in that church. I'm a member. If the church undertakes an endeavor that I don't like or in a style I don't like, I'm going to show up at a business meeting and express my opinion, especially if I'm a dues-paying member." Membership has been about entitlement for far too long. That age is gone; it's over. The postmoderns will not buy this. We never should have, and they are calling us to task for it.

Membership is defined now by participation. I'm a member here because I am here. I'm a member because I worship here. I'm a member because I'm engaged in a small group. I'm a member not because I signed on the dotted line but because you know my name and you know to count on me, as long as I still consider you my tribe. That's the crucial factor. Membership is going to be a fluid concept, and we're going to be affected by that.

The new generation will change the way we measure giving. Young adults will give, but they won't give to big-bucket budgets. They will give to specific needs and opportunities, but it has to be something they can see for themselves. They can and should learn to tithe, but the church's budget is going to start to look a whole lot different. There may not be anything in it for literature, unless it's for children. You may invest a whole lot more in Web technology. There may not be a lot of denominational missions giving when they can give money to the shelter down the street. We may not have a big building campaign.

They're going to accomplish the work of the church differently. They aren't going to head up committees. They will work in teams, and you won't know who the leader is because the work is shared. If they show up at business meetings at all, they will ask awkward questions like, "Jesus didn't do this, so why are we?" They will tell the story of the gospel differently. A major task for future leaders is going to be finding ways to connect and keep connected this demographic who doesn't see an institution as something central to their lives or well-being.

Some people who stay up late at night and study these things say that we are in a cultural cycle and in due time the cycle will come back around. I'm not so sure. I think we have experienced a tsunami of change that has fundamentally altered the contours of the North American culture and the church with it. I don't think things will ever go back to the way they used to be. For instance, we have seen a changing of national denominational structures. They are losing their influence in the life of the local church. For one thing the world is shrinking, and we can do missions through our local church. And second, if the local church can do the mission work itself, it only follows that soon the church will give their support directly to the mission work, bypassing the large national structures of the denominations.

We are witnessing a sea change in the church not unlike the Reformation. In the first Reformation, Martin Luther led the people to pull authority back to themselves from the church. Now ministry itself is being pulled away from the professional clergy and done by those who have been ordained to do the work because their love for Christ was evident. I don't think we will ever go back to the way church used to be. I am the pastor of a megachurch. This has huge implications for me. Don't think I haven't given it a lot of thought and prayer.

I don't think it should frighten us that we haven't figured it out. No one else seems to have figured it out either. Music companies can't figure out how to make money in this wired world. Theaters can't figure out how to stay in business as more and more people have their own theater systems in their homes. The church figured out what to do when Rome fell. This challenge is going to be just as hard.

What Cannot Change

What's important is that we hang onto the essentials of Christianity. Kairos is a work in progress, but I don't want to give you the impression that there aren't essentials. Some things will have to be deconstructed to reach this generation—salesmanship evangelism, the linear teaching model, allegiance to an institution. But methods are not sacred. Buildings are not sacred. The space where you meet is significant but only as it provides an environment in which the people meet with God and connect with one another.

The Kairos space is created with those intentions—the tables, the coffee-house atmosphere, the low lighting. You enter in the back, which is key, because you can get in without much notice. How deep you come in or how much you participate is always up to you.

When we want to encourage participation in prayer, we set up stations for this. We bring in comfortable chairs, rugs, little areas where you can curl up and journal, or quiet corners where you can be alone before God. We don't do this stuff because it's cool. We do it because it's inviting. We do it because it connects people to Christ.

We are intentional about connecting them to Christ, starting where they are and then growing them toward a balanced, mature faith walk. This is where the essentials come in. At Kairos we call it "the three-legged stool": worship, discipleship, and service.

We want them to be involved in worship, public and private. You should be constantly surprised by the presence of God, responding in awe, thanksgiving, and confession. Some experiences are too big for you to respond to by yourself. You need brothers and sisters to sing and shout with you and for you. Some experiences of grief and lamentation you can't carry by yourself. This is why we worship together.

In Kairos services we baptize. Sometimes we are baptizing them into Brentwood Baptist Church, but sometimes people are being obedient to get baptized and then go to a different church. We've had to deconstruct baptism, asking ourselves, "What are the essentials?" The Kairos requirement for baptism is a profession of faith, confirmed by one of our counselors. Baptism is about confession and obedience, not church membership.

Our second goal is to get them into a discipleship group. We want them to be involved in personal Bible study. This is an essential. You have to do this on your own, and it should be part of your daily life, but you also need to do it in some kind of accountability group. Accountability is especially crucial to this demographic, and it's a huge challenge to make it happen.

The third leg is service. Some things you only learn by doing. Some lessons Jesus will teach you only by obedience. And you need to be out there engaging the culture, telling your story, being of service to others. The interesting thing is that you can start with any leg of this stool, and it will lead you to the others.

It's got to be more than just cool lighting, incense, and coffee. These people are hustled and manipulated all day. They can tell the difference. They may not know why, but their radar will start pinging.

Where Do I Begin?

When people ask us how to begin a Kairos, we tell them these are the key ingredients:

1. prayer as strategy
2. the consistent leadership of a pastor
3. Bible-based teaching
4. authentic, trustworthy worship leadership
5. the environment you create
6. lay leadership

Once you have all those elements in place, these are necessary for long-term success:

1. savvy marketing to the demographic once you have something that is up and working
2. support of church leaders, such as the governing body and the resource allocators
3. missions opportunities
4. pastoral care
5. small-group discipleship/accountability

Finally, I can tell you from experience where you must begin: you must love them.

Come Over to Macedonia and Help Us

I did not need to go looking for a ministry. I had one. But Kairos came at a unique moment in time for me, a particularly important time.

With the growth of Brentwood Baptist, we were becoming increasingly burdened with all the things you have to do to run a big church: meeting with city planners, dealing with growth consultants, working on goals and strategies. I didn't get into the ministry because I am a particularly gifted CEO or strategist. I got into it for the pure joy of telling somebody else about Jesus in a way that would allow a person to respond to what Christ has done in my life and can do for them. The irony of success like BBC's is that you can get so busy running the church that preaching is the last thing you get to give your attention to. Studying becomes another item on your to-do list.

Kairos has a rawness, a nakedness to it. It has no frills, no dancing ponies. There is simply, "Here's what the Bible says. Here's what it means to you." Recently we talked about Daniel in the lion's den. This might have been one of the Bible stories they heard as kids. They had no idea Daniel could teach them how to live right now. They had no idea that Daniel was going to teach them about prayer—not crisis prayer but constant prayer because we live in the lion's den. That's what the apostle Paul was trying to tell us, why he said we should pray without ceasing.

When I started teaching these things at Kairos, they were all new lessons to these young people. I had forgotten what happens when you simply tell the truth of the gospel. I had almost forgotten that people are starving to hear it.

As challenging as it might be, we in the local church have to find a way to reach this demographic. We have no choice. We must reach them because, as I reminded one of our charter members, if we don't reach them, we will have the unique privilege of giving birth to a church and burying it in the same lifetime. But above all we need to reach them because these are the ones Jesus told us we must reach—the outcasts, the captives, the poor in spirit, and the orphans. We have no option here; the local church is going to have to develop a missional attitude toward this people group if the local congregation is going to succeed in reaching them. This isn't a new model. Missions is the original model. We are called to be a missionary people.

When I was growing up in church, missions was a big deal. Missionaries were the heroes of our faith. Sometimes, it seemed to me, the more you loved Jesus, the further from home you would go. I have recently discovered that you can receive your own "Macedonian call" and not have to leave your current zip code. My Macedonia isn't that far away. It's located at the other end of our building every Tuesday night.

Remember Lottie Moon? She baked cookies for the children of her neighborhood in China. That was the point of her connection. I drink lots of coffee. I've learned to text. This must be our task: we must study culture because Jesus chose to live in culture. And that is where the God of creation chose to manifest himself—within time and space. Culture is the language of our lives. If you are going to speak to people, you must learn their language. This is one of the most crucial ways we demonstrate that we love as God loves: we come to them. We don't ask them to come to us.

When people call me and say they want to start a Kairos ministry, I tell them, "Tell me how you are praying." Don't tell me what you want to do. Tell me how you are praying. Is this something that is coming out of that kind of intense prayer where you finally get quiet enough to hear God's heart? Is that where your desire to begin a Kairos is coming from? Or do you simply want to be "relevant"? Have you seen something that somebody is doing that is attracting young adults, and you're thinking, *We've got to do what they're doing?* That motivation won't work. But if the Lord is breaking your heart for the young adults around you, then Kairos may be one of your answers. It may become your mission.

Cathy Patterson remembers the Tuesday night when a young woman in tears grabbed her and asked if she could speak to her. Her boyfriend had just broken up with her. She didn't know what she was going to do. Cathy was initially afraid this young woman was a suicide risk, so she focused intently on what the young woman was saying, trying to pick up any signal that we might have to take some kind of action. But the young woman kept talking about lots of boyfriends and lots of breakups, of being used until there was nothing left of her inside. This young woman cried so hard and so long that her tears ruined the leather jacket Cathy was wearing. Later that night Cathy walked up to me and said, "We are going to make this work for these kids. Just tell me who I have to go fight, and I'll go fight them, but we are going to make this work." That was her version of the Kairos prayer. The tear-stained red leather jacket hangs in her closet as a constant reminder that God's love compels her to do what she is doing.

Kairos is not a program. It's not a box you can buy and unpack at your church. Kairos is a moment, a unique moment when you know that you, with God's help, have to find a way to reach the young adults in your community who, despite all appearances, really want to tell someone their story. They want someone to love them enough to listen. They are looking for someone who will tell them about Jesus in a way that makes sense in their world. They are our children and grandchildren, the children of our neighborhoods and communities. They deliver your pizza and wait on you at the local mall. They are your bankers and insurance agents, all brand-new in their careers.

And they are lost. Do you know what it is to be lost? It means you don't know where you are, how you got there, or how to get to where you want to go. Lost people can't find their way home. Like rescue swimmers looking over the ocean for someone whose boat has sunk, we don't expect those who are lost to find their way. We have to go to them. When you are sitting somewhere having a cup of coffee and you look around the café at all of the young adults in the room and realize you can no longer sit still, you are going to have to find a way to reach them, then it will be Kairos for you. The time will be right for you and uniquely your own.

In that moment, know that I've been praying for you.

Lord Jesus,

Do you know my kids? I call them kids because I am old enough to be their dad. And I call them kids because, well, they are. They have the look of an adult, but inside they are lost, wide-eyed in their confusion.

What can I say to them? I am a stranger in their world. I don't blog. I'm not in Facebook or on MySpace. I hate to text message. I would rather talk on the phone. I'm not sure I know their world.

I know who You are. I have always known. I haven't always listened, but I have always known. There has never been a time when I didn't know.

I have a father who reads the Bible and prays. Hearing that you love me as a father loves a child wasn't a stretch for me.

I have a mother, strong and committed and always there. But these kids didn't. They have to learn life's lessons from the ground up. What do I tell them?

• • • •

Tell them the truth.

Any life, like any building, is built on the same foundation—stones and concrete and ground that doesn't move.

Tell the truth. Tell them to trust the foundation that will not shake.

*Tell them that no disappointment—no pain, no fail-
ure—can ever tear down what I am building in them.*

Tell them the truth, and the telling will be enough.

Yes, I know your kids.

I have known them all along.

I have never not known them.

I called them, but they didn't recognize my voice.

There was no Eli to tell Samuel to listen.

*There have been many other promises, many disappoint-
ments, too much pain for them to listen one more time.*

But I have never stopped.

Never stopped watching them.

Hurting for them.

Longing for them.

Calling for them.

Watching for them.

Loving them.

I know each one's name.

I know each one's journey step-by-step.

I know their hopes and losses, their joys and tears.

I know your kids.

Tell them.

And the telling will be enough.

Amen.

• • • •

*May there be no shade of difference between what I tell
them and the truth You are.*

Amen.

Notes

1. David Kinnaman and Gabe Lyons, *unChristian: What a New Generation Really Thinks about Christianity . . . and Why It Matters* (Grand Rapids, MI: Baker Books, 2007), 11.

2. N. T. Wright, "The Resurrection and the Postmodern Dilemma," originally published in Sewanee Theological Review 41.2, 1998. Reproduced by the author on his Web site: www.ntwright page.com/Wright_Resurrection_Postmodern.htm.

3. Dallas Willard, *The Divine Conspiracy: Rediscovering Our Hidden Life In God* (New York, NY: HarperSanFrancisco, a division of HarperCollins, 1998), 94.

4. Gary Smalley and John Trent, *The Blessing* (Nashville, TN: Thomas Nelson Publishers, 1986), 24.

5. John Prine, "Angel from Montgomery," sung by Bonnie Raitt (Sour Grapes Music, Inc./Walden Music, Inc., admin by WB Music Corp/ASCAP).

6. Bobby Braddock, "I Wanna Talk About Me," (Sony Music/ATV Songs d/b/a Tree Publishing).

If you would like information on the structure and operations of Kairos, to obtain copies of Kairos leadership materials such as the Kairos Connections Operations Manual, the Kairos Production Team Operations Manual, the Kairos Greeter Teams Manual, or the Kairos Discipleship Manual, or to view our Web resources, contact us at www.kairosnashville.com.